JOSIP BROZ TITO

JOSIP BROZ TITO

Ruth Schiffman

1987
CHELSEA HOUSE PUBLISHERS
NEW YORK
NEW HAVEN   PHILADELPHIA

DR
1300
.S35
1987

EDITORIAL DIRECTOR: Nancy Toff
MANAGING EDITOR: Karyn Gullen Browne
COPY CHIEF: Perry Scott King
ART DIRECTOR: Giannella Garrett
PICTURE EDITOR: Elizabeth Terhune

Staff for JOSIP BROZ TITO

SENIOR EDITOR: John W. Selfridge
ASSISTANT EDITORS: Maria Behan, Pierre Hauser, Kathleen McDermott, Bert Yaeger
COPY EDITOR: Sean Dolan
DESIGN ASSISTANT: Jill Goldreyer
PICTURE RESEARCH: Karen Herman
LAYOUT: David Murray
PRODUCTION COORDINATOR: Alma Rodriguez
PRODUCTION ASSISTANT: Karen Dreste
COVER ILLUSTRATION: Victoria Tomaselli

CREATIVE DIRECTOR: Harold Steinberg

Frontispiece courtesy of AP/Wide World Photos

First Printing

Library of Congress Cataloging in Publication Data

Schiffman, Ruth. JOSIP BROZ TITO

(World leaders past & present)
Bibliography: p.
Includes index.
1. Tito, Josip Broz, 1892–1980— Juvenile literature.
2. Yugoslavia—Presidents—Biography—Juvenile literature.
3. Yugoslavia—History—1918–1945— Juvenile literature.
4. Yugoslavia—History—1945–1980— Juvenile literature.
[1. Tito, Josip Broz, 1892–1980. 2. Heads of state.
3. Yugoslavia—History—1918–1945. 4. Yugoslavia—
History—1945–1980] I. Title. II. Series.
DR1300.S35   1987   949.7′023′0924 [B] [92] 86-31754

ISBN 0-87754-443-3

Contents

ADENAUER
ALEXANDER THE GREAT
MARC ANTONY
KING ARTHUR
ATATÜRK
ATTLEE
BEGIN
BEN-GURION
BISMARCK
LÉON BLUM
BOLÍVAR
CESARE BORGIA
BRANDT
BREZHNEV
CAESAR
CALVIN
CASTRO
CATHERINE THE GREAT
CHARLEMAGNE
CHIANG KAI-SHEK
CHURCHILL
CLEMENCEAU
CLEOPATRA
CORTÉS
CROMWELL
DANTON
DE GAULLE
DE VALERA
DISRAELI
EISENHOWER
ELEANOR OF AQUITAINE
QUEEN ELIZABETH I
FERDINAND AND ISABELLA
FRANCO

FREDERICK THE GREAT
INDIRA GANDHI
MOHANDAS GANDHI
GARIBALDI
GENGHIS KHAN
GLADSTONE
GORBACHEV
HAMMARSKJÖLD
HENRY VIII
HENRY OF NAVARRE
HINDENBURG
HITLER
HO CHI MINH
HUSSEIN
IVAN THE TERRIBLE
ANDREW JACKSON
JEFFERSON
JOAN OF ARC
POPE JOHN XXIII
LYNDON JOHNSON
JUÁREZ
JOHN F. KENNEDY
KENYATTA
KHOMEINI
KHRUSHCHEV
MARTIN LUTHER KING, JR.
KISSINGER
LENIN
LINCOLN
LLOYD GEORGE
LOUIS XIV
LUTHER
JUDAS MACCABEUS
MAO ZEDONG

MARY, QUEEN OF SCOTS
GOLDA MEIR
METTERNICH
MUSSOLINI
NAPOLEON
NASSER
NEHRU
NERO
NICHOLAS II
NIXON
NKRUMAH
PERICLES
PERÓN
QADDAFI
ROBESPIERRE
ELEANOR ROOSEVELT
FRANKLIN D. ROOSEVELT
THEODORE ROOSEVELT
SADAT
STALIN
SUN YAT-SEN
TAMERLANE
THATCHER
TITO
TROTSKY
TRUDEAU
TRUMAN
VICTORIA
WASHINGTON
WEIZMANN
WOODROW WILSON
XERXES
ZHOU ENLAI

ON LEADERSHIP
Arthur M. Schlesinger, jr.

LEADERSHIP, it may be said, is really what makes the world go round. Love no doubt smooths the passage; but love is a private transaction between consenting adults. Leadership is a public transaction with history. The idea of leadership affirms the capacity of individuals to move, inspire, and mobilize masses of people so that they act together in pursuit of an end. Sometimes leadership serves good purposes, sometimes bad; but whether the end is benign or evil, great leaders are those men and women who leave their personal stamp on history.

Now, the very concept of leadership implies the proposition that individuals can make a difference. This proposition has never been universally accepted. From classical times to the present day, eminent thinkers have regarded individuals as no more than the agents and pawns of larger forces, whether the gods and goddesses of the ancient world or, in the modern era, race, class, nation, the dialectic, the will of the people, the spirit of the times, history itself. Against such forces, the individual dwindles into insignificance.

So contends the thesis of historical determinism. Tolstoy's great novel *War and Peace* offers a famous statement of the case. Why, Tolstoy asked, did millions of men in the Napoleonic wars, denying their human feelings and their common sense, move back and forth across Europe slaughtering their fellows? "The war," Tolstoy answered, "was bound to happen simply because it was bound to happen." All prior history predetermined it. As for leaders, they, Tolstoy said, "are but the labels that serve to give a name to an end and, like labels, they have the least possible connection with the event." The greater the leader, "the more conspicuous the inevitability and the predestination of every act he commits." The leader, said Tolstoy, is "the slave of history."

Determinism takes many forms. Marxism is the determinism of class. Nazism the determinism of race. But the idea of men and women as the slaves of history runs athwart the deepest human instincts. Rigid determinism abolishes the idea of human freedom—

the assumption of free choice that underlies every move we make, every word we speak, every thought we think. It abolishes the idea of human responsibility, since it is manifestly unfair to reward or punish people for actions that are by definition beyond their control. No one can live consistently by any deterministic creed. The Marxist states prove this themselves by their extreme susceptibility to the cult of leadership.

More than that, history refutes the idea that individuals make no difference. In December 1931 a British politician crossing Park Avenue in New York City between 76th and 77th Streets around 10:30 P.M. looked in the wrong direction and was knocked down by an automobile—a moment, he later recalled, of a man aghast, a world aglare: "I do not understand why I was not broken like an eggshell or squashed like a gooseberry." Fourteen months later an American politician, sitting in an open car in Miami, Florida, was fired on by an assassin; the man beside him was hit. Those who believe that individuals make no difference to history might well ponder whether the next two decades would have been the same had Mario Constasino's car killed Winston Churchill in 1931 and Giuseppe Zangara's bullet killed Franklin Roosevelt in 1933. Suppose, in addition, that Adolf Hitler had been killed in the street fighting during the Munich *Putsch* of 1923 and that Lenin had died of typhus during World War I. What would the 20th century be like now?

For better or for worse, individuals do make a difference. "The notion that a people can run itself and its affairs anonymously," wrote the philosopher William James, "is now well known to be the silliest of absurdities. Mankind does nothing save through initiatives on the part of inventors, great or small, and imitation by the rest of us—these are the sole factors in human progress. Individuals of genius show the way, and set the patterns, which common people then adopt and follow."

Leadership, James suggests, means leadership in thought as well as in action. In the long run, leaders in thought may well make the greater difference to the world. But, as Woodrow Wilson once said, "Those only are leaders of men, in the general eye, who lead in action. . . . It is at their hands that new thought gets its translation into the crude language of deeds." Leaders in thought often invent in solitude and obscurity, leaving to later generations the tasks of imitation. Leaders in action—the leaders portrayed in this series—have to be effective in their own time.

And they cannot be effective by themselves. They must act in response to the rhythms of their age. Their genius must be adapted, in a phrase of William James's, "to the receptivities of the moment." Leaders are useless without followers. "There goes the mob," said the French politician hearing a clamor in the streets. "I am their leader. I must follow them." Great leaders turn the inchoate emotions of the mob to purposes of their own. They seize on the opportunities of their time, the hopes, fears, frustrations, crises, potentialities. They succeed when events have prepared the way for them, when the community is awaiting to be aroused, when they can provide the clarifying and organizing ideas. Leadership ignites the circuit between the individual and the mass and thereby alters history.

It may alter history for better or for worse. Leaders have been responsible for the most extravagant follies and most monstrous crimes that have beset suffering humanity. They have also been vital in such gains as humanity has made in individual freedom, religious and racial tolerance, social justice and respect for human rights.

There is no sure way to tell in advance who is going to lead for good and who for evil. But a glance at the gallery of men and women in *World Leaders—Past and Present* suggests some useful tests.

One test is this: do leaders lead by force or by persuasion? By command or by consent? Through most of history leadership was exercised by the divine right of authority. The duty of followers was to defer and to obey. "Theirs not to reason why,/ Theirs but to do and die." On occasion, as with the so-called "enlightened despots" of the 18th century in Europe, absolutist leadership was animated by humane purposes. More often, absolutism nourished the passion for domination, land, gold and conquest and resulted in tyranny.

The great revolution of modern times has been the revolution of equality. The idea that all people should be equal in their legal condition has undermined the old structure of authority, hierarchy and deference. The revolution of equality has had two contrary effects on the nature of leadership. For equality, as Alexis de Tocqueville pointed out in his great study *Democracy in America*, might mean equality in servitude as well as equality in freedom.

"I know of only two methods of establishing equality in the political world," Tocqueville wrote. "Rights must be given to every citizen, or none at all to anyone . . . save one, who is the master of all." There was no middle ground "between the sovereignty of all and the absolute power of one man." In his astonishing prediction of 20th-century totalitarian dictatorship, Tocqueville explained how the revolution of equality could lead to the *"Führerprinzip"* and more terrible absolutism than the world had ever known.

But when rights are given to every citizen and the sovereignty of all is established, the problem of leadership takes a new form, becomes more exacting than ever before. It is easy to issue commands and enforce them by the rope and the stake, the concentration camp and the *gulag.* It is much harder to use argument and achievement to overcome opposition and win consent. The Founding Fathers of the United States understood the difficulty. They believed that history had given them the opportunity to decide, as Alexander Hamilton wrote in the first Federalist Paper, whether men are indeed capable of basing government on "reflection and choice, or whether they are forever destined to depend . . . on accident and force."

Government by reflection and choice called for a new style of leadership and a new quality of followership. It required leaders to be responsive to popular concerns, and it required followers to be active and informed participants in the process. Democracy does not eliminate emotion from politics; sometimes it fosters demagoguery; but it is confident that, as the greatest of democratic leaders put it, you cannot fool all of the people all of the time. It measures leadership by results and retires those who overreach or falter or fail.

It is true that in the long run despots are measured by results too. But they can postpone the day of judgment, sometimes indefinitely, and in the meantime they can do infinite harm. It is also true that democracy is no guarantee of virtue and intelligence in government, for the voice of the people is not necessarily the voice of God. But democracy, by assuring the right of opposition, offers built-in resistance to the evils inherent in absolutism. As the theologian Reinhold Niebuhr summed it up, "Man's capacity for justice makes democracy possible, but man's inclination to injustice makes democracy necessary."

A second test for leadership is the end for which power is sought. When leaders have as their goal the supremacy of a master race or the promotion of totalitarian revolution or the acquisition and exploitation of colonies or the protection of greed and privilege or the preservation of personal power, it is likely that their leadership will do little to advance the cause of humanity. When their goal is the abolition of slavery, the liberation of women, the enlargement of opportunity for the poor and powerless, the extension of equal rights to racial minorities, the defense of the freedoms of expression and opposition, it is likely that their leadership will increase the sum of human liberty and welfare.

Leaders have done great harm to the world. They have also conferred great benefits. You will find both sorts in this series. Even "good" leaders must be regarded with a certain wariness. Leaders are not demigods; they put on their trousers one leg after another just like ordinary mortals. No leader is infallible, and every leader needs to be reminded of this at regular intervals. Irreverence irritates leaders but is their salvation. Unquestioning submission corrupts leaders and demands followers. Making a cult of a leader is always a mistake. Fortunately hero worship generates its own antidote. "Every hero," said Emerson, "becomes a bore at last."

The signal benefit the great leaders confer is to embolden the rest of us to live according to our own best selves, to be active, insistent, and resolute in affirming our own sense of things. For great leaders attest to the reality of human freedom against the supposed inevitabilities of history. And they attest to the wisdom and power that may lie within the most unlikely of us, which is why Abraham Lincoln remains the supreme example of great leadership. A great leader, said Emerson, exhibits new possibilities to all humanity. "We feed on genius. . . . Great men exist that there may be greater men."

Great leaders, in short, justify themselves by emancipating and empowering their followers. So humanity struggles to master its destiny, remembering with Alexis de Tocqueville: "It is true that around every man a fatal circle is traced beyond which he cannot pass; but within the wide verge of that circle he is powerful and free; as it is with man, so with communities."

1

Escaping the Ring

On a frigid winter day in March 1943, a small man in a simple woolen uniform walked along the steep banks of the Neretva, a turbulent mountain river in western Yugoslavia. His fierce gray eyes and sallow-cheeked face bore an expression of concern and determination suggesting the perilous situation his army faced. The man, Josip Broz Tito, and the guerrilla force he commanded, the Partisans, were surrounded. Formed by the Yugoslav Communist party (YCP) in 1941 to resist their nation's occupation by Nazi Germany, the Partisans had grown from a ragtag band of mountain fighters into an army of 20,000 uniformed regulars representing every element of Yugoslavia's diverse ethnic and religious mixture. Initially armed with the most primitive equipment — clubs, axes, and old hunting guns — the insurgents had captured a substantial stockpile of tanks, explosives, and guns in deft hit-and-run operations against the less mobile Germans. Perfecting the art of the surprise attack, they had retaken much of Bosnia — a province in the central western part of the country that the Germans referred to as "Titoland."

> *Experts do not usually take sufficient account of the strength of the human will. If human beings are determined to do something, they will do it, even if all calculation shows it to be impossible.*
> —JOSIP BROZ TITO

Josip Broz Tito, dressed in the uniform of the Partisans. As secretary general of the Yugoslav Communist party (YCP), Tito formed the Partisan guerrilla army in 1941 to resist Yugoslavia's occupation by Italy and Germany.

SOVFOTO

UPI/BETTMANN NEWSPHOTOS

Yugoslav children give the communist salute in 1943. Tito formed the Partisans intending not only to harass the occupying forces but to expand communist power — toward the eventual goal of establishing a new, revolutionary government in Yugoslavia.

Now is our chance to beat the communists to their knees. If we don't take it, it may be the worse for us.

—DRAŽA MIHAJLOVIĆ
commander of the Četnik
forces, at the beginning
of the German
Fourth Offensive

But now a huge enemy offensive threatened not only the Partisans' territorial gains but their very existence. The Fourth Offensive, also known as Operation White, combined Adolf Hitler's Nazi army with Slavic and Italian armies — with which the German leader had divided up the conquered country after invading on April 6, 1941. Tito's forces had been driven out of Bosnia into Hercegovina, a region to the south. While four German divisions approached from the north and east, three Italian divisions took up positions in the south and west.

On the snowy slopes of Mount Prenj, directly across the Neretva River from where Tito stood, were 15,000 Četniks, former officers in the Royal Yugoslav Army, with whom the Partisans were engaged in a civil war. The Četniks had initially fought alongside the Partisans, but they had begun to collaborate with the Germans after their leader, Draža Mihajlović, and Tito could not agree on a proper strategy for resisting the brutal Nazi occupiers. Seeking to avoid fierce reprisals, Mihajlović had opposed direct attacks on the Germans. He had become especially cautious after the infamous October 1941 Kragujevac slaughter, when 2,600 Yugoslav civilians were executed in retaliation for a Partisan raid that killed 26 Nazi soldiers. As the representative of the deposed Yugoslav head of state, King Peter II, and of the exiled government in London, Mihajlović was concerned mostly with ensuring the postwar reinstatement of the monarchy. He accurately suspected that Tito, as head of the YCP, planned to use the chaotic circumstances of the war to try to install a communist government based on the model of the Soviet Union.

As Tito paced outside the headquarters he had established in a water mill, his troops were setting up camp along the Neretva valley. The soldiers were trying to recover from an exhausting 100-mile march they had made immediately following the Nazi's launching of Operation White. The Partisans were suffering greatly from bitter cold and hunger. In the rugged mountains of Hercegovina and Bosnia, vegetation was scarce, so for the most part troops survived on boiled mutton from thin sheep driven in front of the army as it marched. With no fruits or green vegetables available, many soldiers attempted to combat scurvy (a disease caused by a lack of vitamin C) by eating young beech leaves or pressing the juice out of beech bark.

To acquire needed supplies and to avoid almost certain annihilation by a superior army, Tito would have to break through the enemy ring and shift his forces to another part of the country, where he could resume the attack. He had done so successfully earlier in the war. But this time, he faced a formidable array of foes, and he had to make sure that none of the 4,500 wounded troops and countless civilian refugees in his forces were left behind. Hitler had ordered his troops to kill all prisoners.

As Tito walked along the river mulling over his options, he was joined by a young aide, Vladimir Dedijer. The two were dressed in identical uniforms — each with a cap adorned by a gold star and a hammer and sickle — a sign of Tito's willingness to share everything equally with his troops. When his troops moved, he moved with them; when they made arduous marches across rough terrain, he shared the burden. His men knew that if one of them was wounded, Tito would risk his life to save him from enemy fire. When there was enough of a lull in the

UPI/BETTMANN NEWSPHOTOS

German soldiers on patrol in a Yugoslavian town during the Nazi invasion of the country, launched on April 6, 1941. Tito's homeland became the 13th nation to fall to Adolf Hitler's forces, following intense air raids on Belgrade, its capital city, and less than two weeks of ground combat. After starting World War II by attacking Poland in 1939, Hitler soon took much of Europe.

A Nazi poster offers a reward of 100,000 reichsmarks (about $40,000) for Tito's capture. Though the Germans clearly understood Tito's value to the Allied cause, Great Britain and the United States ignored Tito until late in the war. Most of the Allied aid went instead to the Četniks, the enemies of Tito's Partisans in the Yugoslav civil war.

Нове мере против бандитизма

наїрада од 100.000 рајхсмарака у злату!

UPI/BETTMANN NEWPHOTOS

fighting to set up headquarters, he accepted whatever accommodations were available — caves, huts, shelters made out of branches in the forest. As the two men walked, however, it was clear from Tito's determined step, from his direct gaze, from the concentrated energy in his compact frame, that, despite the identical uniform, he was the true leader. He had formed the Partisans in 1941, after having been the secretary general of the Yugoslav Communist party, working clandestinely during the 1930s to overthrow the monarchy. As military commander, he had put aside temporarily his dream of forming a communist state and had shown tremendous ability as a tactician and soldier. The Germans recognized him as the heart and soul of the Partisan movement and plastered thousands of posters around Yugoslavia offering 100,000 reichsmarks for Tito's capture.

As the two men continued up the river valley, they saw Partisan troops scurrying to retrieve their wounded from the recent 100-mile march. Though deeply concerned about his army's predicament,

Tito was always calm and collected in a crisis. He slowly revealed to Dedijer a series of documents that underscored a further Partisan difficulty — lack of foreign support. The Soviet Union, which had offered guidance to the YCP before the war and encouraged the formation of the Partisan army, had again refused to send military aid. "Is it really impossible after twenty months of heroic, almost superhuman fighting to find some way of helping us?" Tito had wired Soviet leader Joseph Stalin ten days after Operation White began. In response, the Soviets had offered moral support but no material assistance.

Tito suddenly explained to Dedijer that during his walk he had conceived a strategy for escaping the ring. It was an ingenious plan. The weakest link in the enemy lines was clearly the Četnik army, which had been racked by dissension, alcoholism, and disorganization. But to have sufficient time to cross the Neretva into Četnik territory without receiving severe damage from the rear, the Partisans had

A map showing the six republics in the Socialist Federal Republic of Yugoslavia — Slovenia, Croatia, Serbia, Montenegro, Macedonia, and Bosnia-Hercegovina. Each is home to one main ethnic group, except Bosnia-Hercegovina, which is made up of Serbians and Croatians. In March 1943 Tito hoped to escape enemy encirclement by shifting his forces from Bosnia-Hercegovina to Montenegro.

SOVFOTO

Members of the Partisan army. Tito's troops used sabotage and hit-and-run attacks against the Nazis, who had more troops and also had an air force, paratroop units, and heavy artillery at their disposal.

somehow to fool the enemy into thinking the movement would be in the opposite direction, northward, against the Germans. Tito decided that to disguise his intentions he would destroy all the bridges along the Neretva. Next, he would send part of his forces north to fend off the Germans and further convince them to expect a full attack in that direction. After drawing the enemy's attention, most of this detachment would swing back to the Neretva and rejoin the rest of the troops. The Partisans would then gather their wounded, create a new bridge, and cross the seventy-yard wide river into Četnik territory. Their goal would be Yugoslavia's southwesternmost province, Montenegro.

Dedijer was impressed but not surprised by his leader's plan. Tito had always come up with bold solutions to seemingly impossible problems. On March 3, 1943, the operation began. First, Partisan engineers blew up several bridges on the Neretva. Then the Partisan First, Second, and Seventh divisions, led by Tito himself, attacked the Germans along a 12-mile front using 15 tanks previously captured from the Italians. It was a direct foray into the heart of the enemy's firepower — something the Partisans usually avoided. The Germans were much better trained, much better equipped, and had the enormous advantage of air support. But against the worst conceivable odds, the attack succeeded. As one Partisan recounted, "Our attack went in like a hurricane. The battle lasted all night. The first two assaults failed, but the third could not be stopped. We swept down like an avalanche." The Germans were pushed back 10 miles, giving the Partisans breathing room. The Germans were also deceived: "The intention of the enemy," said a German intelligence report of March 5, "is to break out to the north."

On the night of March 6, 1943, Tito again stood above the raging waters of the Neretva. He had given the order for his Second Division to cross a decimated railroad bridge and establish a foothold on the other side of the river. From where Tito stood, he could see an enemy pillbox from which Četnik soldiers were sending harassing fire. "That's a job for volunteers. Six men with hand grenades and submachines," he commanded. At midnight, a daring band of Partisans crawled over the twisted iron wreckage of the half-submerged railroad bridge. Each carried a grenade in his teeth. They crept up on the pillbox and dumped in two grenades. Within minutes, all the Četniks inside were dead. Partisan engineers, linked by ropes, quickly set to work threading an improvised wooden plank bridge through the misshapen girders of the old bridge. More troops were rushed across, and after some fierce fighting, a five-mile wide area was secured.

At dawn the next morning Tito called to his men, "Start the crossing." Thus began the monumental task of moving 25,000 Partisans, many of them

The remains of one of the several bridges on the Neretva River that Tito ordered his engineers to destroy in March 1943 in order to disguise the intended direction of Partisan movement. Tito's army eventually did cross the Neretva, as some 20,000 soldiers and about 4,500 wounded made their way over a makeshift wooden span in the midst of intense enemy fire.

EASTFOTO

Tito sits alongside fellow Partisan Ivo Ribar, after being wounded in the Nazi Fifth Offensive of June 1943. Tito was known for sharing every bit of fighting and hardship with his troops. During the "Battle of the Wounded," he demonstrated tremendous courage and resourcefulness, traits he would later display for 35 years as communist leader of Yugoslavia.

wounded, across the flimsy bridge in the midst of intense enemy bombardment. Since none of the heavy equipment the Partisans had captured could be transported across the ramshackle span, trucks and tanks were sent crashing into the wild river below. By the second day the entire Second Division was across and the movement of the wounded began. Many of the wounded were forced by the steady barrage of enemy fire to crawl across on all fours. Some were carried by prisoners of war. Occasionally, after a bomb jarred the bridge, a mule carrying a wounded man would lose its footing, and both would tumble into the froth below.

Tito stood on the bank, watching with tears in his eyes, not flinching as German planes swooped by, strafing close to him. "If Stalin had only sent a few antiaircraft guns," he lamented to an aide. Some planes knocked out sections of the bridge, and Partisan engineers scrambled to keep it patched together. Though the enemy fire became heavier, Partisan morale remained remarkably high, according to Dedijer's account. He recalled one civilian refugee, a shepherd boy from Sandzak, who was even joyful during the crossing. "It is true they are bombing us mercilessly here," the boy had said. "But here are six planes dropping bombs. It means six bombers less on the Eastern [Russian] Front. And the victory will be achieved sooner." On March 11 Tito and his staff crossed the river. Partisans in the north were desperately holding off the Germans, who had captured the key town of Prozor and were advancing quickly. Pressure mounted from all sides. But by dawn on March 14, the last of the wounded were taken across, and the next day they were followed by the last of the rearguard. The Germans finally reached the Neretva on March 17, but the Partisans were gone, having left, in the words of the German commander, Alexander von Lohr, "neither booty, nor prisoners, nor dead behind them."

But the "Battle of the Wounded" was far from over. The Partisans still had to make their way up the jagged limestone crags of the 7,000-foot Mount Prenj and battle the Četniks. As they crept up the snow-covered slopes, they were under constant fire from artillery, mortars, and machine guns. The Partisans suffered terribly; many died from typhus. Others collapsed from hunger. "Some died where they were sitting from sheer exhaustion," Tito would recall later. At one point, more than a thousand Partisans were trapped between two peaks, blocked on the sides by deep snow and in front by slow-moving wounded. But eventually the Partisans overcame the Četniks, primarily because of desertions in the Četnik ranks. Many Četniks became disillusioned with the idea of joining with the Nazis to fight fellow Yugoslavs; whole battalions defected to the Partisan cause. Within a week, the Partisans would be in Montenegro.

On top of Mount Prenj, an exhausted Tito surveyed with a mixture of sadness and relief the usually picturesque Neretva valley, now choked with brown battle clouds. As always, Tito had distinguished himself in battle as a hardy soldier and a brilliant strategist, helping the Partisans elude the German Fourth Offensive as they had three earlier ones. Throughout the rest of World War II, Tito would display the same combination of cunning, stamina, and physical courage that he demonstrated at Neretva. His leadership would enable the Partisans to survive a number of equally difficult campaigns and to recapture much of their homeland as the Nazi war machine weakened and the Allies, especially Great Britain and the United States, became more generous with aid. The Partisans' tremendous success in the face of extreme adversity would win them the enduring affection of their countrymen, and Tito's name would become known around the globe. His wartime heroics would secure him a position as leader of Yugoslavia for 35 years, during which time he would show his resourcefulness and independence in rebuilding his shattered country, in installing a communist government, in rebuffing attempts by the Soviet Union to dominate his nation, in helping to found the movement of nonaligned countries, and in creating a revolutionary new form of communism that would take his name—"Titoism."

EASTFOTO

A Četnik soldier. Former members of the Royal Yugoslav Army, the Četniks began to collaborate with the Germans after their leader, Draža Mihajlović, could not agree with Tito on a strategy for resistance. In March 1943, during what would later be called the "Battle of the Wounded," Tito chose to direct his main attack against the Četniks and escape to southern Yugoslavia.

2

Apprenticeship

In the years before World War I, life was hard in the little village of Kumrovec in western Croatia, then a province in the Austro-Hungarian Empire, now part of Yugoslavia. It was particularly hard for the peasant family of Franjo Broz and his wife, Marija. Of their 15 children, 8 had died from malnutrition or from the constant epidemics of diphtheria, scarlet fever, and other diseases. On May 25, 1892, Marija gave birth to a son, whom the Brozes named Josip. Though he survived the early childhood diseases, Josip would almost die from an attack of diphtheria when he was 10 years old.

The Broz family had a sheepdog named Polak, of whom the children were particularly fond. Most of them in fact had learned to walk by grasping hold of his thick hair while gentle Polak walked around the room, dragging them along after him. But one winter, when the little 15-acre farm on which the Broz family lived had not produced enough food, let alone a surplus to pay for such things as fuel, Franjo Broz decided to sell Polak to an official on a nearby estate in return for firewood. Despite the children's pleas, the deal was completed, and Franjo took Polak away to live with his new owner. However, even before Franjo returned home, Polak had escaped and returned to the children. Sternly, the father trudged off again with the reluctant dog. But again Polak escaped. This time the children hid him in a nearby cave in the woods. After two weeks the adults gave up and Polak stayed with the children.

My childhood was difficult. There were many children in the family and it was no easy matter to look after them. Often there was not enough bread, and my mother was driven to lock the larder while we children received what she considered she could give us, and not what we could eat.
—JOSIP BROZ TITO

Slavic peasant woman and child. In 1892 Josip Broz (Tito's given name) was born into a peasant family in the Slavic region of Croatia, then a territory in the Austro-Hungarian Empire. In the poor village of Kumrovec, the Brozes were considered relatively wealthy, though their farm measured only 15 acres, and their seven children often went hungry.

It was taken for granted in my village that by the time a child was seven he was already a productive worker. I drove the cattle and helped hoe the corn and weed the garden and, I remember so well, turned the heavy grindstone that made our grain into flour.

—JOSIP BROZ TITO

The village of Čenkov, one of the many places Broz lived during his extensive travels around the Austro-Hungarian empire from 1907 to 1913. During that time he worked as a waiter, a mechanic, and a locksmith. Observing the freedoms enjoyed by other citizens of the empire, Broz began to resent the treatment of Croatians as second-class citizens.

For the rest of his life Josip Broz — or Marshal Josip Tito, as he eventually became known when he was the leader of Yugoslavia — would fondly recall the episode as a way of describing the harshness of peasant life in the areas of the Austro-Hungarian Empire that were inhabited primarily by Slavs — those peoples, including the South Slavic Slovenians, Croatians, and Serbians, who are bound by related languages. After World War I, the southern regions of the Austro-Hungarian Empire would be merged with part of the Slavic territories once controlled by the Ottoman (Turkish) Empire and the independent Slavic state of Serbia to form Yugoslavia, "land of the South Slavs."

Broz later recalled his childhood home. "We shared the house with a cousin," he said. "The hall was used by both families; on either side of the hall were two rooms. An open-hearth kitchen, where there was always a stock of firewood, was also shared." The nine members of the Broz family therefore were squeezed into two rooms. Remarkably, they were considered one of the richest families in Kumrovec.

Josip received his only formal education at the village school, starting at age seven and finishing five years later. The school had just one teacher for its 350 pupils.

EASTFOTO

Despite the hardships, these were not entirely miserable times for young Josip. He was particularly happy, he later recalled, when he was able to visit his mother's father in Slovenia, another Slavic territory in the Austro-Hungarian Empire. (Slovenia is now the northernmost province of Yugoslavia.) The old man seems to have made a favorite of Josip, a light-eyed blond like himself and his daughter. Josip took great pleasure in helping tend his grandfather's horses. He became a skilled rider known for his ability to break even the most difficult steeds. He would never lose his love of well-bred horses. As a guerrilla leader during World War II, when he depended on horses to give his small army mobility against the Germans, Josip would always take care to dismount when climbing hills to lighten the horse's load.

While still a child, Josip became aware of political issues, especially the fact that Croatia was treated poorly by its Austro-Hungarian rulers. For example, all the railway stations in the province were run by Hungarians. Croatians had to ask in Hungarian for tickets or they would not get them. It was for this reason, when Josip was 11, that some Croatian patriots in a nearby village removed the Hungarian flag from the station. Police were called, and shots were fired during the ensuing confrontation. By the time the uprising was quelled, 26 people had been killed and more than 3,000 Croatians had been arrested. As punishment, each family in the area was ordered to house four members of the Hungarian army for a month. The Broz family spent the next four weeks hungrier than ever, while four hulking Hungarian soldiers ate the bulk of the household's meager food supply.

Because of such conditions, thousands of Croatians emigrated to the United States during this period. Franjo Broz, anticipating a barren future for his son, hoped that Josip would be one of the emigrants. But the dream died when Franjo could not raise the $100 fare for his son.

Instead, in 1907 the 15-year-old Josip left his native village for the nearby town of Sisak. He had thought at one time of learning to be a tailor, for he

EASTFOTO

Broz (at left in second row, with cap) stands with fellow metalworkers at a Slovenian factory in 1912. In the years before World War I, Broz gradually became involved in unions campaigning for higher wages and better working conditions — often losing his job as a result.

liked the look and feel of fine garments. But, influenced by reports of the money to be earned from tips, he became a waiter instead.

This job did not last long. After a few months, Josip became friends with some locksmiths, who convinced him to join them in the trade. Locksmiths were important at that time, for as Croatia began to industrialize, their mechanical knowledge was useful in helping to keep factories running and agricultural machinery moving. Their skills were needed for much more than simple locks and keys.

Josip's training included two evening classes each week. It was in these classes, during the three years he served as an apprentice, that he discovered the wealth of information to be learned from books. One book that greatly impressed him was Edward Bellamy's *Looking Backward*, a political novel about a socialist utopia. From magazines he learned about worker movements throughout the world and what they were trying to do to improve the lives of laborers and peasants. Young Broz considered it unfair that in his whole village only three men were educated enough to vote. Illiteracy and ignorance, he felt, kept the villagers in poverty. It was at this time that he began to consider the necessity of broad social change.

By the time Broz was 18, he was determined to see more of the world and moved on to the nearby city of Zagreb, the capital of Croatia. With the help of friends, he managed to get a job there as a locksmith and soon had joined a metalworkers' labor union. But after several months, feeling restless, he headed for Trieste, a port city on the northern shore of the Adriatic Sea. Even further disappointment awaited him there; he could not find a job, and after living for a while on an allowance from the union, he moved back to Zagreb. There he found work with a man who repaired bicycles and automobiles. He also became more deeply involved in the affairs of the Metalworkers Union. Its members, he learned, now wanted to institute unemployment compensation programs and to provide small pensions for the elderly.

The annual May Day parade was the union's forum for calling attention to these demands, which many groups in Croatia opposed. The Roman Catholic church, for example, actively discouraged its members from taking part in the parade. Priests warned their flocks that anyone who marched would go to hell. In some towns the parades provoked violence, but in Zagreb the workers were not harassed. However, as they walked through the city, Broz saw a small boy pointing to one of the marchers and saying loudly: "Look, Mother, there is our father among the devils." The union's militancy increased, and the workers at the factory where Broz was employed struck for higher wages. They were partly successful, but by that time Broz was ready to move again. Encouraged by his employer, who had taken a liking to him, he decided to seek his fortune in the more advanced factories of Austria and Germany. It was a roundabout route he took. He worked at a series of jobs in small towns and cities where he frequently participated in strikes and demonstrations, often losing his job as a result.

Eventually Broz ended up in Vienna, the Austrian capital, where he went to work in an automobile factory outside the city. There he learned to repair engines and to test-drive finished automobiles. Life was not all work and union activity, however. On his days off, Broz would often go to a Viennese music hall called the Orpheum, which featured magicians and clowns and popular music. He also found time to learn ballroom dancing, becoming adept at the waltz but having trouble with other popular dances of the time, the quadrille and the polonaise.

It was at this time, in 1913, that Broz turned 21 and returned home to serve his compulsory time in the Austro-Hungarian army. Army service was rigorous, made worse by archaic customs. Recruits were required, for example, to memorize the lengthy names of all the members of the Austrian royal family. If a soldier could not recite the names on demand, he would face a severe beating. The officers, men from aristocratic families, did nothing to prevent the noncommissioned officers from dealing as

It was an army of oppression, which not only held my people in subjection but served as an instrument to enslave other nations. Moreover, it was an old-fashioned and unintelligent army. It operated by rule and formula and, instead of teaching men how to fight, taught them how to drill.
—JOSIP BROZ TITO
describing the
Austro-Hungarian army,
into which he was
drafted in 1913

Gavrilo Princip (right), the Serbian nationalist who assassinated Archduke Franz Ferdinand, the heir to the Austrian throne, in Sarajevo, Bosnia-Hercegovina, on June 28, 1914. With him are other conspirators in the Balkan plot that prompted Austria, with German backing, to declare war on Serbia, thus beginning World War I.

meanly and pettily as they chose with the largely ignorant peasant recruits. Broz would later say that the army taught the men "not how to fight, but how to drill."

Then, in 1914, everything changed. One day the soldiers were called to the parade ground and told that on June 28 Archduke Franz Ferdinand, heir to the throne of Austria, and his wife had been assassinated by a Serbian extremist, Gavrilo Princip, while visiting the city of Sarajevo. Serbia, a country to the southeast of Croatia, won its independence from the Ottoman Empire in 1878 and had sought to assert its leadership over the Slavic peoples of the Balkan Peninsula, many of whom, including the Croatians, were subjects of the Austro-Hungarian Empire. The archduke was known to have opposed Serbia's ambitions. His murder greatly worsened the already bitter relations between Austria-Hungary and Serbia. Austria-Hungary issued an ultimatum to Serbia that contained several terms, one of which was to punish Princip's confederates. Serbia, supported by Russia, agreed to some of the demands but refused others. Austria-Hungary was adamant, and on July 28, as Serbia continued to resist, the empire declared war on its tiny neighbor. Within a few days, World War I was in full fury, with

Germany and the Ottoman Empire on the Austro-Hungarian side and Russia, Britain, France, Italy (and eventually the United States) supporting the Serbs.

Josip Broz's sympathies were with the Serbs, and when he expressed them publicly he was thrown into a military prison. But since Austria-Hungary was in dire need of manpower, he was subsequently released and rejoined his unit in time to fight in the Carpathian Mountains against the Russian invasion of Hungary. By the time Broz caught up with them, his comrades were trying to repulse the Russians just 120 miles from Budapest, the Hungarian capital. From the start Broz was a skillful soldier, and he soon was promoted to command a platoon.

The line of battle remained unchanged for most of that winter, but in the spring the Russians launched a surprise offensive. In a battle on Easter Sunday, 1915, Broz was badly wounded; a Russian cavalryman's double-pronged lance had pierced his back just below his left arm. When he recovered his senses, he found himself a prisoner of war in a Russian military hospital near the ancient city of Kazan on the Volga River. There he began a long period of illness and convalescence. At one point in the hospital, weakened from pain and infection, he developed pneumonia and became delirious. In his hallucinations he raved at an icon near his head, shouting that the saint was trying to steal his belongings.

THE BETTMANN ARCHIVE

Austrian sharpshooters firing on Serbian positions in 1914. After hostilities broke out, Broz expressed support for Serbia, sympathizing with that nation's desire to unite all South Slavic regions, including Croatia. Though jailed briefly for his views, Broz was soon fighting for the Austro-Hungarian army on the eastern front against Russia.

Eventually he recovered and was well enough to move about. He learned Russian in order to be able to work, even though as a prisoner of war he was not required to do so. His first job outside of the prison camp was in a nearby town, where he kept the mill going by repairing its defective parts. When that project ended in the winter of 1916–17, Broz was set to work with other prisoners of war repairing the Trans-Siberian railroad. The men worked in the bitter cold, even though they lacked proper clothing. Their pay was never enough to buy sufficient food. Every day one of the weaker members of the crew succumbed to the conditions. Broz, who had become a recognized leader among the prisoners, protested the ill-treatment. He was sent back to prison and while there received a beating from three Cossacks that he was to remember for the rest of his life.

The war was going disastrously for the Russian army. In 1916 alone, 1 million Russian troops had died in fruitless campaigns. The German army, even though it was simultaneously fighting the British, French, and Italians on the western front, was just too well supplied, too well armed, and too well led for the Russian forces, and in March 1917, the disintegration of tsarist Russia reached its final phase. Workers and soldiers in Petrograd, the Russian capital, mutinied and rioted. Tsar Nicholas II was forced to abdicate. A provisional government under Prince Georgi Lvov was formed, but revolutionary agitation persisted as various groups competed for power. The liberal members of the Duma, or parliament, wanted to break up the great estates of the nobility

Soldiers guard the Trans-Siberian railroad, which, as a Russian prisoner of war, Broz was forced to repair during the harsh winter of 1916–17. Though a skilled soldier, Broz had been captured in the spring of 1915 after receiving a severe wound in the back from a Russian soldier's lance.

and apportion them among the peasants. The liberals believed that with this incentive the peasants, many of whom had refused to fight for the hated tsar, might resume the struggle against the German invaders. Radical deputies from the Petrograd Soviet (council) of Workers' and Soldiers' Deputies wanted the war ended immediately.

In the background, but gaining influence, were members of a radical socialist group called the Bolshevik party, including Vladimir Lenin, who, on April 16, 1917, had returned to Petrograd from exile in Switzerland. His passage through wartime Germany had been assisted by the Germans, who, seeing him as a potential troublemaker for the Russian government, had provided him with a special sealed train. As the quarrel between the liberals and socialists worsened, Lenin decided that it was time to strike. On July 16 he attempted to seize power. But the attempt was premature and many of the Bolsheviks, including Leon Trotsky, one of the party's leading spokesmen, were arrested. Lenin himself fled to Finland. But the sequence of events had totally undermined Prince Lvov, leading to his resignation on July 20. The new provisional government was led by the moderate socialist Aleksandr Kerensky.

At this time, Broz, released from prison, was also in Petrograd (later to be renamed Leningrad) urging workers not to fight for the Kerensky government.

A communist activist distributes newspapers in Moscow in February 1917, by which time Russia had been decimated by war — suffering massive food shortages and greater casualties than any other nation. In such conditions, Marxism — a political and social theory that called for a workers' revolution — made great gains in its appeal to Russian laborers.

Tito had seen the [Russian] Revolution triumph and the working class seize power. He had seen, or so he believed, the Future—the Future for Russia and the whole world. He had found a cause by comparison with which family, religion, fatherland counted as nothing. Henceforth he had but one aim: to bring about a communist revolution in his own country.
—FITZROY MACLEAN
British liaison to the Partisan army during World War II and biographer of Tito

31

TASS FROM SOVFOTO

V. I. Lenin, the Russian revolutionary who founded the Bolshevik party in 1903. His substantial contributions to Marxist theory included the idea that communism could be implemented in countries lacking a large working class. He proposed that rule by the party — a vanguard of professional revolutionaries — could temporarily be substituted for dictatorship by the proletariat.

He was arrested for his activities and imprisoned in the cellar of a rat-infested fortress, where he slept on the floor with only damp straw for bedding. After three weeks he was exiled to the Ural Mountains — the edge of Siberia. But he managed to escape from the train carrying him there during a stopover at Ekaterinburg (now called Sverdlovsk).

Eventually he reached the Siberian city of Omsk, where he learned that the Bolshevik revolution had succeeded. Lenin had overthrown Kerensky's government in November and had opened peace talks with Germany.

As Broz saw it, Lenin's communist regime of the newly formed Soviet socialist republic promised a better way of life for workers and peasants. Broz soon got the chance to defend this belief. He joined the Red Army, the Bolshevik defense force, in the civil war against the Whites, a coalition of liberals, former nobles, and ethnic minority groups opposing the measures advocated by Lenin and Trotsky. While with the Red forces, Broz read much about Lenin and Trotsky and discussed their teachings with the other soldiers. But in all the time that he was in Soviet Russia, he would later recall, he did not once hear the name of the man who was to figure so importantly in his life, Joseph Stalin.

At first the Red cause did not flourish in Siberia. The Reds were driven out of Omsk, and Broz took refuge in a village 35 miles outside the city, populated mostly by seminomadic Kirghiz people. The Kirghiz were so impressed by Broz's way with horses that their chief presented him with a valuable mare, which he named Mercedes. In addition, he acquired a couple of dogs, including a wolfhound. After some months, he was able to return to Omsk, where he resumed his courtship of a 16-year-old girl he had met there earlier. Her name was Pelagea Byelusnova, and her parents were a working-class couple whom Broz had met when he had first arrived in the city. Within a few days, in January 1920, Josip and Pelagea were married. Shortly thereafter, the couple began a long journey to a new Balkan nation, of which Croatia had been made a part. But when they reached Croatia, Broz once again was thrown

in jail, having been denounced as a Bolshevik. He was released a few days later and made his way back to his native village. On reaching Kumrovec at the beginning of October, he surprised his father and brothers at supper. He found out that his mother had died two years earlier. Two days after arriving at Kumrovec, Pelagea gave birth to a son. Tragically, however, the infant died within days. The young couple left the village and moved to Zagreb.

War, prison, and revolution had toughened and enlightened the young man who had been drafted into the Austro-Hungarian army. Also, a different Zagreb awaited him. It was no longer a city subject to foreign whims but was part of a new country. Josip Broz was a devoted Slav nationalist, but he was also convinced that in Soviet Russia he had glimpsed a way to create a better world. In Soviet Russia he had come to believe that a worker's state was possible. That was what he now wanted for his own country.

Rebels in Petrograd fire on a tsarist police stronghold in March 1917. The spontaneous uprising of Russian workers and soldiers that grew out of opposition to the war resulted in the abdication of Tsar Nicholas II. The so-called "March Revolution" was followed by a struggle for power between the provisional government, made up of former members of the Russian parliament, and more radical groups.

33

3

A New Life in a New Nation

During the war, Serbian leaders had met in London with representatives of the Austro-Hungarian Slavic territories of Croatia and Slovenia, and the groups had agreed to direct their war efforts toward the formation of an independent nation combining all South Slavs. After the collapse of the Austro-Hungarian Empire following its defeat in World War I, their dream became a reality. On December 4, 1918, the Kingdom of the Serbs, Croats, and Slovenes (the original name of Yugoslavia) was formally proclaimed at a joint congress in Zagreb. In addition to Slovenia, Croatia, and Serbia, the new nation included the Slavic regions of Montenegro, Bosnia, Hercegovina, most of Dalmatia, and part of Macedonia. A diverse mixture of religions, cultures, and ethnic groups came together in the new kingdom. Four Slavic languages — Serbian, Croatian, Slovenian, and Macedonian — and three non-Slavic ones — Albanian, Hungarian, and Turkish — were spoken. Serbo-Croatian, an amalgam of the closely-related Serbian and Croatian languages, was established as the country's official language. The country's ethnic groups tended to follow separate

> *The new state was created without reference to the people, who were never asked what kind of state it should be, how relationships among the different nationalities should be settled, whether it should be a republic or a kingdom, or what social organization should be adopted.*
> —VLADIMIR DEDIJER
> Yugoslav Communist party member and biographer of Tito, on the formation of the Kingdom of the Serbs, Croats, and Slovenes in 1918

A view of Zagreb, the capital of Croatia. Determined to bring Marx's vision of a classless society to his native land, Broz returned to Zagreb with his Russian wife, Pelagea, in 1920. On December 4, 1918, Croatia had become part of a new nation, the Kingdom of the Serbs, Croats, and Slovenes.

religious faiths. Slovenes and Croatians were mainly Roman Catholic; Serbians were Serbian Orthodox; many Bosnians were Muslims; and Macedonians were Greek Orthodox. The Serbians, with 5 million of the kingdom's 12 million inhabitants, became the dominant national group — contributing the king, Peter Karadjordjević, and many military leaders. In addition, the country's capital, Belgrade, and the seat of its national church, the Serbian Orthodox Church, were in Serbia.

Many of Croatia's 3 million inhabitants felt that the largely Orthodox Serbians had been given too much power. Besides being separated by different religions, the two groups were also distanced by a different cultural heritage. While Croatian traditions had developed under the influence of the West, Serbian customs had derived from those of its Turkish rulers.

In addition, Croatians were upset that their leaders, who had been instrumental in the formation of

The Kingdom of the Serbs, Croats, and Slovenes (renamed Yugoslavia in 1929) was a melting pot of nationality groups, languages, cultures, and religions. Through most of history, the kingdom's new states had been administered separately by various conquering empires and had thereby acquired distinct national identities.

SOVFOTO

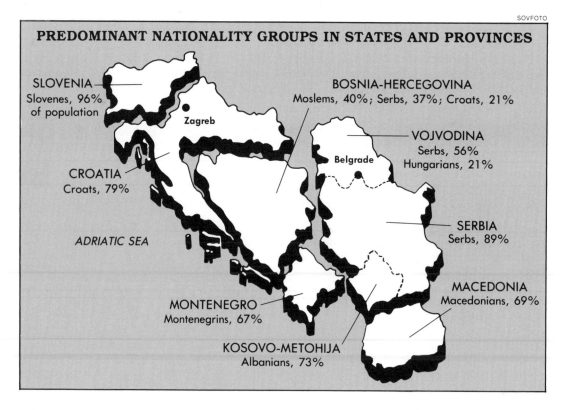

PREDOMINANT NATIONALITY GROUPS IN STATES AND PROVINCES

SLOVENIA
Slovenes, 96% of population

Zagreb

CROATIA
Croats, 79%

ADRIATIC SEA

BOSNIA-HERCEGOVINA
Moslems, 40%; Serbs, 37%; Croats, 21%

Belgrade

VOJVODINA
Serbs, 56%
Hungarians, 21%

SERBIA
Serbs, 89%

MACEDONIA
Macedonians, 69%

MONTENEGRO
Montenegrins, 67%

KOSOVO-METOHIJA
Albanians, 73%

the new country, had been frozen out of its government. A long dispute over how to supplement the monarchy in a new government had ended with the adoption in 1921 of a constitution providing for a strong central government, which would favor the majority Serbians. While the centralist plan called for a single-chamber parliament and a strong executive, the Croats had advocated a federalist solution allocating greater power to the regional governments. Out of this resentment emerged the Croat Peasant party, which was organized by Stjepan Radić with the goal of establishing a separate Croatian state. The erratic Radić was jailed repeatedly, and he eventually agreed to join the government. The Kingdom of the Serbs, Croats, and Slovenes would officially become Yugoslavia in October 1929.

Alexander, the son of King Peter, inherited the throne in 1921. Though a stubborn and courageous man with a strong sense of duty, he seems to have been a monarch more of the 19th than the 20th century. He not only paid himself a large salary, but he appropriated banks and businesses for his own use. For Alexander, constitutional guarantees were a fiction to quiet the peasants, who clamored for a voice in government.

Many Yugoslavs were unwilling to accept this state of affairs. Among them was the Yugoslav So-

Serbian street scene. Serbia, which as an independent kingdom had provided the major impetus for the unification of the South Slavs, became the new country's largest region and most powerful nationality group. While some radical Croatian groups focused on lessening the influence of the Serbian-dominated central government, Broz and the fledgling YCP, founded in 1920, concentrated on the larger goal of a communist state.

cialist Workers party, which in June 1920 became the Yugoslav Communist party (YCP). The change of name was more than a formality; it indicated a change of political direction. The reborn party agreed to ally itself with the Communist International, or Comintern, an organization formed by Lenin in 1919 to coordinate an international network of communist parties. Josip Broz, the man who many years later would rupture the YCP's alliance with Moscow but who was then working as a mechanic in a Zagreb workshop, joined the local Croatian branch of the party in 1921.

Soon thereafter, the party ran a list of candidates in the election for delegates to the country's constitutional convention. The Communists did better than they expected. Fifty-nine of their candidates won seats, giving the party the third largest delegation among the 12 groups that had fielded candidates. Within a year, the government passed a law making membership in the YCP illegal. Communist deputies were expelled from the constitutional assembly. The ousted deputies and all other Communists were now outlaws, liable to arrest and imprisonment.

Like many of his colleagues, Broz went underground, using his renewed membership in the Metalworkers Union as a cover for his party activities. Leaving Zagreb, he and his young wife went to the small village of Veliko Trojstvo, where he found employment in a small mill. It did not take much of his time, and the long free periods were spent chatting with peasants waiting for their grain to be processed. It was a ready-made opportunity for someone as skilled at political work as Broz was.

At a worker's funeral, Broz spoke of ways to relieve the poverty of the workers. He was arrested when a Catholic priest objected to what he considered the desecration of a religious ceremony. But an Orthodox priest, who had no fondness for the Catholics, coached Broz for his court appearance. The argument convinced the judge, and he dismissed the charges.

Josip and Pelagea lived near the mill for more than four years. Two children were born to them there, but both died in infancy. The local carpenter who made the coffins for the two infants felt so sorry for the grieving couple that he did not charge them.

Despite his personal tragedies, Broz was rising steadily in the party ranks. Most of the party's high officials lived abroad in order to avoid arrest. Direction of party affairs therefore was left to the local officials, and Broz took advantage of this situation. He traveled to nearby towns and villages, encouraging workers to form clandestine party cells. It was risky work, as the government continued to crack down on Communists. During this time, Moša Pijade, an artist and intellectual who was to be a long-time associate of Broz, was arrested for publishing a communist newspaper. The king decided to make an example of Pijade and had him sentenced to 20 years in prison. Only a severe sentence, the king argued, would deter others from spreading dissent.

There was some good news for Broz, however. Finally, in 1924, a strong and healthy son was born to him and Pelagea. The child was named Zarko. The good news, however, was followed by an unfortunate event. Shortly after Zarko's birth, the mill owner died, leaving the plant to his son. The new owner was less tolerant of Broz's political activities and fired him.

In autumn of 1925, at the suggestion of party colleagues, Broz moved his family to Krajevica, a little seaport on the northern Adriatic. There Broz soon found himself in the middle of a labor dispute. The workers claimed that the plant management was holding back the men's wages, to use as capital. This forced the workers to buy food on credit, always at higher prices than if they had been able to pay cash. The management claimed that the company's main client, the navy, had not paid its bills, leaving the shipbuilders with no money to pay the men. To strengthen the worker's cause in the dispute, Broz had organized them into a union as soon as he arrived. To back up their demands, he then led them out on strike. The workers' anger increased when they learned that the company had lied; the navy had been paying its bills all along. After nine days, management capitulated and paid the workers. But

EASTFOTO

A forged identity card with which Broz presented himself as I. Kostanjšek, qualified engineer. In the 1920s, as Broz became increasingly involved in the outlawed YCP, he was forced to adopt several aliases and to change jobs continually. He worked in a flour mill, in a shipyard, and in a railway repair shop, in each place leaving behind a flourishing party cell.

King Alexander, who ruled Yugoslavia from 1921 to 1934, and his wife, Princess Maria of Romania. Historians have described Alexander as stubborn, austere, and courageous. The years of his reign were marked by an increasingly bleak economic situation and growing public protest against the king's despotic policies.

THE BETTMANN ARCHIVE

His is undoubtedly the most interesting personality in this trial. His face makes you think of steel. His light grey eyes behind his spectacles are cold, but alert and calm.

—a Soviet journalist, reporting on Tito's trial in November 1928

a few days later Broz was fired.

Once more, in October 1926, the Broz family moved to Zagreb, taking with them Josip's library. A voracious reader with a special interest in social and political theory, he had built up a large collection of books and lent them to anyone who expressed an interest. This habit would later get him sent to prison when one of his books was found in the home of a young worker accused of being a revolutionary. Broz remembered the judge asking: "What do the workers need to read scientific books for, when their job is merely to chop things with an axe or hit them with a hammer? Why should they get interested in politics?"

But Josip Broz was most certainly interested in politics, and in 1927, when he was 35, he became a full-time Communist party official when he was named the YCP secretary of the Zagreb branch of the Metalworkers Union. Now he had to travel extensively throughout the country, a difficult task that he sought to make easier by using a variety of aliases. During this time Jirachek, Gligorejević, Zagorac, and Mekas were just some of the false names he used to disguise his movements. He also varied his official occupations, becoming at various times a barber, an engineer, and even a businessman. At one time, despite not knowing a word of English, he traveled on a passport that said he was a naturalized British subject of Croatian extraction.

These were grim times in Yugoslavia. In 1928 Yugoslavs worked for the lowest wages in Europe. Farm prices had been falling steadily, impoverishing the peasants. Broz would later remember an instance when three peasant families had to combine their incomes to have enough to buy a box of matches.

So many trade-union officials were arrested for trying to change these conditions that Broz took on the duties of secretary to a leather workers' union in addition to his post with the metalworkers. He was very busy. "I had plenty of work to do," he recalled. "A strike in a shoe factory, a strike in a metal workshop, signing contracts with the employers in the name of the trade unions, organizing help for arrested trade-union members, plus my party work."

In February 1928, at a clandestine Communist party conference in Zagreb, Broz led a dissident group in overthrowing the old leadership of the party branch. He was elected the new secretary of the Zagreb party.

Then began a life on the run. An informer led the police to Broz. For the first time he was charged with a serious crime — membership in the Communist party. Broz was defiant. In court, at the beginning of November 1928, he not only admitted his communist affiliations but also declared that he did not recognize the authority of the court to try him. He was sentenced to five years in jail.

The police crackdown that had proved to be Broz's undoing was just the first of many repressive measures now taken by the Yugoslav king and government. During the first week of 1929 King Alexander revoked the constitution of 1921. He dissolved Parliament, banned all political parties, and imposed press censorship. Yugoslavia's last democratic institutions were swept away with an autocratic wand.

These peasants traveled to Belgrade in 1923 to present gifts to the newborn crown prince of Serbia. Such pomp and ceremony could not disguise the true state of affairs in Yugoslavia — food shortages were rampant, prices were skyrocketing, royal troops were often needed to quell strikes and riots. The YCP, torn by factional strife over the nationalities question and hampered by government repression, could not capitalize on the popular discontent.

41

4

"University"

Josip Broz was sent to a prison near the area where he had grown up. Life was hard there — even for someone raised in poverty. The day's food was a small loaf of bread in the morning and a bowl of thin soup in the evening. Broz shared a cell with seven other men who established a rough form of socialism among themselves. Though cigarettes were a rare treat, the four smokers in the group shared every cigarette they got their hands on. If a cigarette came their way, one of them would mark it into fourths, and each would smoke the section marked off for him.

All the prisoners were expected to work. On a typical day, Broz would be given a large sack of goose feathers to be cleaned by evening or rolls of brown paper that had to be cut and pasted into bags. For this he would be paid — at a time when five *dinars* bought a pack of cigarettes — three and a half dinars a month.

But Broz's mechanical skills rescued him. The prison power plant needed constant attention, and the warden assigned Broz to keep it running. Not only did he now have interesting work but also freedom of movement. In the power plant, he was able to cement his friendship with Moša Pijade, who,

> *I believe that natural laws are higher than those created by one class to oppress another. I am even prepared to sacrifice my life for my ideals.*
> —JOSIP BROZ TITO
> at his trial in November 1928

Portrait of Josip Broz taken in 1928. After becoming secretary of the Zagreb branch of the YCP in February of that year, Broz made several daring escapes to avoid police capture. Finally arrested in August, he was sentenced to five years in prison for his communist beliefs.

In Leopoglava jail, Broz (right) organized a communist party organization. He also continued his education by reading hundreds of books and discussing politics with other Yugoslav revolutionaries, including Moša Pijade (left), a Jewish intellectual from Belgrade.

although his term had been shortened to 14 years, still faced a long period behind bars. He had been named Broz's assistant.

Pijade was a well-educated man and had wide knowledge of Marxist theory. In some ways he acted as Broz's teacher, recommending books for him to read to supplement his meager formal education. Since political books were forbidden, Pijade also showed Broz how to conceal them from the guards. Karl Marx's *Das Kapital* (*Capital*), for example, could be hidden inside the jacket of a copy of *The Arabian Nights*. Eventually, as his own background in Marxist theory became stronger, Broz joined with Pijade in teaching other, less knowledgeable communists in the prison. Afterward, Broz would say that the five-year term he spent in the prison was "just like being in a university."

An unexpected benefit of the power-plant job was that Broz could occasionally get outside the prison. A woman who owned a nearby tavern often asked the warden to send an electrician to repair broken appliances. The woman was sympathetic to the revolutionary cause, and after Broz came to her inn, she agreed to help him. Each time he came, supposedly to fix an electrical appliance, she would distract his guard with a drink. Meanwhile, Broz would be in an upstairs room, holding a clandestine meeting with other communists. At this time there were about 3,000 members of the YCP, but fewer than 1,000 were inside the country — most of the leadership had fled to Vienna to avoid persecution. Therefore, Broz's continued contacts with party members were crucial.

As might be expected, Broz's time in prison profoundly affected his family life. Soon after Broz was imprisoned, Pelagea and her son were sent back to the Soviet Union, on the orders of the party. It was to be a permanent separation.

Eventually the time came for Broz to go free. He had served his sentence. But, in typical fashion, he did not want simply to walk out the door. First, before he was released, he asked the warden to let him grow his hair longer. He wanted to avoid having his close-cropped convict's haircut betray where he had spent five years. In addition, he sought permission to have a prison tailor make him a new suit from cloth that a friend had sent him. Broz would always strive to look his best, and years later his carefully tailored braided uniforms and the diamond ring that he always wore would be the symbols of a man who insisted on being an unorthodox Marxist.

If prison was Broz's university, then the five years afterward were his internship, spent in the field, practicing what he had learned from Pijade and his books. At the time of his release from prison in 1934 he was 42 years old and a dedicated Communist revolutionary. He knew that he would be constantly watched. To disguise himself, he dyed his hair red, grew a mustache, and put on eyeglasses. He collected passports and identity cards that testified to a dozen new names and occupations.

In Zagreb, Broz joined the YCP's provincial committee for Croatia, which ordered him to go to Austria for a meeting with the exiled central committee of the YCP, the party's ruling body. Broz crossed the border disguised as a member of a Slovenian walking society.

Karl Marx, the German political philosopher and founder of modern socialism, whose seminal work, *Das Kapital*, Broz read in prison. Marx argued that class struggle in the capitalist system between the proletariat and the bourgeoisie would inevitably lead to a more mature stage of development: a classless society in which the state, the church, and the concept of private property would become obsolete.

EASTFOTO

UPI/BETTMANN NEWSPHOTOS

Becoming a high party official after his release from prison, Broz traveled to Slovenia in 1934 to set up a party conference and there recruited Edvard Kardelj (pictured here in 1945, when he was Yugoslavia's foreign minister). Then a young schoolteacher, Kardelj impressed Broz with his dedication, his efficiency, and his even temperament.

Reaching Vienna, he appeared before the central committee to report on conditions in the Yugoslav nation and in the Yugoslav party. Broz bluntly told the committee members that the country was in turmoil and the party was in disarray. Its biggest problem, he said, was that the members in Yugoslavia had to face continual persecution and danger and felt estranged from the leadership, which was relatively safe in exile. It must have been a convincing performance, because soon after Broz was appointed a member of the national party leadership. Then, late in August 1934, he was sent back to Yugoslavia to organize conferences in Slovenia and Croatia.

In Slovenia, Broz met another of the young communists who would be closely associated with him in the momentous years ahead. This was Edvard Kardelj, a schoolteacher, who had already undergone brutal police torture for his political beliefs.

Kardelj was impressed with Broz. He said, "We found him very direct of speech and manner. He was in his early forties, about 20 years older than we were, and looked it. But he was nothing like the old party leaders. When you asked him a question, he did not always come back at you with a quotation from Marx, Engels, or Lenin. Instead, he spoke in practical, commonsense terms."

It was about this time that Broz began to use a new name. It was the custom for revolutionary agitators, as part of their disguise, to use pseudonyms. The custom had been established by such luminaries in the communist movement as Vladimir Ulyanov, who became Lenin, and Josef Dzhugashvili, who became Stalin. At first Broz fancied using the name Rudi but found someone else was already using it. For no particular reason he then chose to be called Tito. It was a common name in Croatia but had no revolutionary significance.

The political situation in Yugoslavia had been in turmoil for some years. Since the end of World War I, Croatian nationalists, led by Radić and encouraged by Yugoslavia's Roman Catholic neighbors, Hungary and Italy, had been agitating for a greater say in the Yugoslav government. As part of this ag-

Dr. Ante Pavelić, leader of the Ustaša, a terrorist organization dedicated to the establishment of an independent Croatian state. On October 9, 1934, a revolutionary with ties to the Ustaša assassinated the tyrannical King Alexander, who had suspended the Yugoslav constitution and dissolved the parliament more than five years earlier.

itation, a semisecret terrorist organization, the Ustaša, was formed. Tensions had come to a boil in June 1928 when Radić was assassinated. Croatian demands for autonomy were refused by King Alexander, who in January 1929 had established his dictatorship. For the next three or four years there had been endless unrest, with the Ustaša continuing to threaten the king. Their leader, Dr. Ante Pavelić, for example, distributed a flier addressed to Alexander. It said: "You may hide yourself, you gypsy, but wherever you go, we will find you and kill you." On October 9, 1934, the prophecy was fulfilled. King Alexander was assassinated by a revolutionary with ties to the Ustaša.

The upheaval that followed was especially dangerous for the communists, and Tito was instructed to leave Yugoslavia at once. He headed for Austria, but upon arriving there found out that he had instead been assigned to work in Moscow as a member of the Balkan secretariat of the Communist International.

47

5

In Stalin's Shadow

When Tito arrived in Moscow in January 1935, the Soviet leader was Joseph Stalin, who had risen to power after Lenin's death in 1924. Stalin had defeated his principal rival for power, Leon Trotsky, and had spent the next dozen years solidifying his position and carrying out a brutal transformation of Soviet society.

The Communist International, or Comintern, had been founded in Moscow in 1919 with the avowed purpose of helping to foster world revolution. Originally the Comintern had been seen as a central clearinghouse for coordinating the activities of the world's communist parties. Under Stalin that had quickly changed; the Comintern had become Stalin's vehicle for subjugating and controlling all non-Soviet communist parties, including the Yugoslav party.

During Tito's first stay in Soviet Russia during the revolution, he had not visited Moscow, but he had taken home glowing reports of the part of the country that he had seen. Now things seemed to be different. Nevertheless, he did not complain. Tito put the changes down to a temporary problem. The temporary internal matter, it would later be revealed, involved the summary execution of thousands, if not millions, of Russians, the wholesale deportation of millions more, the forcing of millions of peasants onto collective farms, and the imposition of one of the world's most terrible dictatorships.

I was excited at being back, but soon my excitement began to cool off. I saw things that were quite different from what I myself had so enthusiastically described in Yugoslavia.
—JOSIP BROZ TITO
on returning to the
Soviet Union in 1935

Russian peasant women. In 1935, after the assassination of King Alexander prompted Yugoslavia to implement drastic security measures, Broz, who began using the name Tito in the mid-1930s, was dispatched by party officials to the Soviet Union to represent the YCP in the Communist International.

Tito was also going through personal turmoil. Pelagea Broz had arrived in Moscow much earlier and had grown apart from her husband. After her husband's arrival in the Soviet capital, she announced her intention to divorce him and marry one of her new friends. Someone who was present said "she was swallowed up in the bureaucratic society."

That summer Tito got his first glimpse of Stalin. At the Seventh Congress of the Comintern, Stalin announced a striking change in Soviet policy. For the time being, Stalin said, revolution must be forgotten. Friendly relations with the Western democracies must be cultivated. Communist parties in other countries must be encouraged to join in popular-front coalitions with noncommunist organizations. In keeping with Stalin's policy, communists were fighting alongside less radical groups against the fascist forces led by General Francisco Franco in the Spanish civil war. One of Tito's tasks at the Comintern was to arrange to send Yugoslav volunteers to fight against Franco. The efforts of communists everywhere, Stalin insisted, must be directed toward mobilizing their countries in a com-

Supporters of the Spanish republic, called Loyalists, guard a barricade in Barcelona during the Spanish civil war, 1936–1939. In 1936 Comintern officials assigned Tito to organize Yugoslav communist volunteers to fight alongside the Loyalists against the right-wing Nationalist forces of General Francisco Franco.

mon goal against the fascist enemy threatening them all, Nazi Germany's Adolf Hitler.

Like the good communist that he was, Tito readily accepted the change in his leader's position. He interpreted Stalin's words to mean that Yugoslav communists must discourage nationalist aspirations among the country's ethnic groups and instead seek unity in the country. They would thus be in a position to help the Soviet Union in the coming fight against Hitler.

But in early 1937 Tito was ready to return home. Along the way he tried to persuade the leading members of the central committee of the YCP that to mobilize the people, they would have to move from Vienna back to Yugoslav soil. Half the committee followed Tito; the remainder moved to Paris.

Back in Zagreb, Tito asked the YCP leaders in Belgrade to send him an aide for his party work. The central committee's choice was Milovan Djilas, who had just been released from prison. In turn, Djilas recruited Ivo Ribar to found a youth organization for the party. Djilas, Pijade, Kardelj, and Aleksander Ranković would for years be Tito's closest confidants. In the end, Djilas would also become one of Tito's harshest critics.

For these young men, these were exciting but confusing times. It is unclear exactly how much Tito and the YCP knew of the political situation in the Soviet Union, but they were apparently aware that Stalin dealt ruthlessly with those who did not conform to his policies and obey the Comintern dictates. It was therefore understandable that when Tito was summoned to Moscow in 1938 he went with great apprehension. Later he said, "I never knew whether or not I would come back alive." But as it turned out, the Moscow visit was a major step forward in his career. He returned to Yugoslavia as secretary general of the Yugoslav Communist party.

One of Tito's first tasks was to insist that the entire party leadership return from its cozy exile in France and Austria. Then, in the summer of 1939, Tito was again summoned to Moscow. There he was confronted with another abrupt change in Stalin's diplomacy. The Soviet dictator had signed a non-

Joseph Stalin, pictured here in 1932, ruthlessly eliminated political opposition following Lenin's death and became absolute ruler of the Soviet Union, leading one of history's harshest regimes for 29 years. Abandoning Lenin's idea of world revolution, Stalin launched a crash process of modernization that transformed a backward country into a leading industrial nation.

Prince Paul (right) chats amiably with Adolf Hitler during the March 1941 meeting at which the Yugoslav leader agreed to join the Germany-Italy-Japan Axis. Paul's accession to the Tripartite Pact enraged his subjects and led to his overthrow, which in turn brought German tanks thundering into Belgrade.

aggression pact with Hitler, giving the Nazi leader a free hand to invade Poland. Within weeks, World War II had begun.

After four months in Moscow, Tito again returned home. For a brief interval, life was happy again. He married for a second time. His bride was a Slovene woman, Herta Has. Within a few months they were the parents of a son, Aleksander.

But international events would soon upset Tito's domestic bliss. Prince Paul, the Yugoslav leader, who had been acting as regent since the death of King Alexander, was drifting toward an alliance with Hitler. Paul's difficult situation was aptly summed up by the British statesman Winston Churchill. The prince, said Churchill, was like "an unfortunate man in a cage with a tiger, hoping not to provoke him, while steadily dinnertime approaches."

In March 1941 Paul endorsed the Tripartite Pact, which linked Yugoslavia officially to Germany, Italy, and Japan. The Yugoslav people rioted. "Better death than the pact," they shouted in the streets of Belgrade. Two days later Prince Paul's regency came to an abrupt end. Prince Peter, Alexander's son and the heir to the throne, was declared legally of age, and a government was formed that included prominent opponents of the Tripartite Pact.

Hitler was furious at this reversal and ordered Yugoslavia destroyed. On April 6, 1941, German troops marched into Yugoslavia, and German bombs rained on Belgrade. One after another the provincial capitals fell. Then, on April 12 Belgrade surrendered. King Peter fled to exile in Britain. On April 17 the Royal Yugoslav Army laid down its arms.

Hitler made Croatia an independent state, headed by Ante Pavelić, the Ustaša leader, who had been long regarded as a puppet of Benito Mussolini, the Italian fascist dictator. In Serbia, another puppet regime was established under General Milan Nedić. Germany and Italy took parts of Slovenia and Montenegro. Italy also received a section of Croatia. Hungary and Albania were thrown token parts of the prostrate Yugoslav state, and Macedonia was handed over to Bulgaria, which had allied itself with Germany. By the end of April 1941 it seemed that Yugoslavia had disappeared forever.

During the German military invasion of Yugoslavia, aptly code-named "Operation Punishment," the Nazi secret police conducted thousands of public executions, including this one in Belgrade's main square. Attempting to break the Yugoslavs' will to resist, the Gestapo also tortured suspected enemies and burned entire peasant villages.

6

Two Wars at Once

By the spring of 1941 Hitler had gobbled up most of Europe; of the major allied powers, France had fallen in 1940, Great Britain was left reeling from a Nazi bombing campaign, and the Soviet Union had just become the victim of a massive German invasion. In June 1941 Tito formed an anti-Nazi guerrilla fighting group known as the Partisans. From the Belgrade house of a businessman sympathetic to the Partisan cause, Tito directed operations. He established contact with Moscow using a shortwave radio but found that since the Soviet Union was itself staggering from the German attack, it was unable to offer more than verbal encouragement. In messages to Moscow, Tito was known by the code name Walter. To his neighbors he was known as Babić. But his soldiers called him Tito, and it was by that name that he would become best known in history. Whatever his name, Tito was an avowed communist and intended to model his army on communist lines. Each newly formed Partisan group had its own political commissar, so that a core of leaders for a communist government would be in place when the time was ripe.

> *This terrible disaster was the result of the criminal policy of the Belgrade rulers, who cared for nothing but their capitalist interests.*
> —JOSIP BROZ TITO
> on the German occupation
> of Yugoslavia in April 1941

In the months following the German attack, Tito (center) gathered his youthful team of Communist party advisers, including the Serbian Aleksander Ranković (left) and the Montenegrin Milovan Djilas (right), and began preparations for an uprising. Ranković and Djilas would later serve in Yugoslavia's postwar communist government.

SOVFOTO

Radé Dedich, a well-known Partisan guerrilla. After Germany attacked the Soviet Union in June 1941, Tito began in earnest to organize a resistance army. The ragtag Partisan bands, which at first were equipped with only axes, clubs, and hunting guns, encompassed every Yugoslav ethnic, religious, and lingual group.

Partisans included members of all Yugoslavia's diverse ethnic groups. Tito himself was a Croatian. His closest aides included Milovan Djilas, a Montenegrin, Moša Pijade, a Serbian Jew, and Edvard Kardelj, a Slovene. An unusual aspect of the Partisan units was that they included large numbers of women. Women served not only in offices and hospitals but also in combat, trained to use the same weapons in the same actions as the men.

In August 1941 Tito advised Stalin that "Partisan operations in Serbia are assuming to an ever greater extent the character of a national uprising. The Germans are holding the larger towns while the villages and hamlets are in the hands of the Partisans."

As the summer ended, Tito left Belgrade to join the fighting. He set up his headquarters in Stolice, a town in the hill country liberated by the Partisans. Not far away, Draža Mihajlović had established the royalist Četnik headquarters. In addition, communist-led Partisan groups were active in Slovenia, Croatia, Bosnia, and Montenegro. At a meeting in Stolice at the end of September, Tito and his aides decided that wherever their fighters gained control of an area, local governments would be replaced by communist national liberation councils. Tito was already looking ahead to the end of the war.

Then, in October 1941 a Partisan brigade ambushed a column of German soldiers outside Kragujevac, a munitions center southeast of Belgrade. Twenty-six Germans were killed, and the Nazis were livid. They declared that the town would pay at the rate of 100 Yugoslavs for every German killed. German soldiers went from house to house, searching for able-bodied men. When they discovered they were 200 men short, they turned to the schools. High school students were rounded up to bring the total of victims to 2,600. The soldiers turned machine guns on the prisoners. Bodies littered the ground. The Germans drove tanks back and forth over the corpses to make sure there were no survivors.

Soon after, Tito and Mihajlović met to discuss possible joint action. But the horrendous outcome of the ambush at Kragujevac had given Mihajlović doubts about whether to cooperate with the aggressive Partisans. In addition, a British liaison officer had been posted to the Četnik camp, demonstrating that the British recognized Mihajlović as the official leader of the Yugoslav resistance. For these reasons Mihajlović was against a merger, and the meeting ended inconclusively.

The Partisans continued to work in obscurity with little support. The press in Britain and the United States (which had not yet entered the war, but was sympathetic to the Allies) praised Četnik actions, while ignoring the Partisans. At the same time, Tito's requests to Moscow for material help brought only encouraging words and no weapons.

Then, on November 1, full-scale fighting broke out between the Partisans and the Četniks. Mihajlović joined his forces with those of the puppet government established in Serbia by the Germans. After that it was a short step until the Četniks were actively helping the Germans hunt down the Partisans. Tito was forced to flee from Stolice.

With the Germans, Serbians, and Četniks all at his back, Tito marched his men west. They reached the safety of a Bosnian mountain town on December

> *It is absolutely essential that you should take all measures to support and alleviate the struggle of the Soviet people. You must start a movement with the slogan of a united front, indeed of a united international front, to fight the German and Italian Fascist bandits. Organize partisan detachments without a moment's delay.*
>
> —JOSEPH STALIN
> Soviet leader, ordering Tito to form a resistance army after the German invasion of the USSR in June 1941

German soldiers search Yugoslavs suspected of guerrilla activities. The Nazis carried out fierce reprisals against Yugoslav civilians in an attempt to curb the Partisans' war of resistance. In October 1941 the Nazis massacred the entire adult male population of Kragujevac, Serbia, in retaliation for a Partisan raid that left 26 German soldiers dead.

With the support of King Peter II's exiled government, Draža Mihajlović (left) created a resistance force called the Četniks out of remnants of the Royal Yugoslav Army. Mihajlović's suspicion of Tito's communist orientation and his receipt of generous Allied aid led him, in 1941, to reject Partisan proposals for cooperation.

UPI/BETTMANN NEWSPHOTOS

> *The time had come to seize power and to seize it in such a way that the bourgeoisie would never regain it.*
> —JOSIP BROZ TITO
> on the formation of the
> Partisan army

24, 1941. It was a long, cold, bloody march made more bitter by the knowledge that wounded comrades left behind were murdered by the Germans.

At this low point in Partisan morale, Tito announced the formation of the First Proletarian Brigade. Like the other Partisans, this elite group would wear red stars on their caps, but superimposed on their red stars, the Proletarian Brigade would have a hammer and sickle in a gesture of solidarity with the Soviet Union.

Not that such gestures seemed to impress Stalin very much. Every time Tito attempted to lay the groundwork for a permanent communist government in Yugoslavia, he encountered opposition from Moscow. Stalin urged that the Partisan army portray itself not as a communist organization but as a coalition of Yugoslavia's many political and ethnic groups. Even after the Četniks turned British weapons on the Partisans, Stalin continued to insist that Tito cooperate with Mihajlović.

The province of Bosnia, now the center of Partisan

activity, had become, in the dismemberment of Yugoslavia by the Axis powers, a Serbian Orthodox enclave in an otherwise Roman Catholic Croatia. Although a Croatian "kingdom" had been established the previous spring, the young Italian prince who had been named as its ruler felt it prudent never to appear there. The actual rulers, Pavelić and his Ustaša army, wanted to eliminate the Serbian minority in their region. In attempting to do so, they were almost as brutal as the Nazis. They desecrated and burned Orthodox churches, killed priests, and slaughtered women and children. The surviving Serbs fled to the hills. There many of them enlisted in Partisan brigades, joining new Croatian recruits who had been disgusted by the excesses of Pavelić's troops.

By January 1942 the Germans were ready to launch their first offensive against the Partisans. With the help of Ustaša ski troops, they drove the Partisans south to Foča, where in relative peace Tito was able to rebuild his forces.

Foča was northwest of Montenegro and had been parceled out to Italy in the dismemberment of Yugoslavia. Djilas was sent to Montenegro to organize action against the Italians. The Montenegrins, always a warrior people, succeeded at first in driving back the Italians. To eliminate the threat, the Italians brought in motorized columns of troops supported by heavy bombing raids.

That situation soon was to change, however. For

Tito (with coat draped about shoulders) reviews the First Proletarian Brigade, an elite unit formed in December 1941 following the Partisans' arduous march from Serbia to Bosnia. Commanding this force was Koča Popović, a one-time surrealist poet whose earlier military experience had been gained as one of the volunteers sent by Tito to fight in the Spanish civil war.

EASTFOTO

EASTFOTO

Tito peruses topographic maps in Bosnia in 1942. Though at first Tito directed Partisan operations from Belgrade, where he was disguised as the upper-class engineer Slavko Babić, he soon joined his troops in the field. His skill as a military tactitian led Gestapo leader Heinrich Himmler to say, "I wish we had a dozen Titos in Germany."

various reasons — according to Tito, "the harsh, sectarian and incorrect attitude" of some of his top aides was largely to blame — the Montenegrins turned against the Partisans. Without the local help on which they had previously relied, the Partisans lost most of their territory by autumn. The Četniks signed an agreement to cooperate with the Italians.

Faced with this setback, Tito himself went to Montenegro. Under his leadership, the Partisans regained much of their lost territory over the winter. But these successes were not enough for Tito, who continued to plead with Stalin for more material assistance. Yet Stalin still sent advice rather than weapons. He told Tito to be less openly communist. He advised cooperation with the Četniks, and he told Tito to use his real name in signing the communiqués.

But Tito and his men kept hoping that eventually the weapons would come. The Russians had promised help, and for 37 bitter nights that winter Pijade and his detachment waited at a prearranged spot for the munitions to be dropped by parachute. The help never came.

The Italians, now assisted by the Četniks, again took control of Montenegro. And worse, from Tito's point of view, the Germans were planning to join in the campaign to eradicate the Partisans. In desperation, he radioed Stalin: "The situation here is critical. Incessant fighting has left the Partisans exhausted. There is no more ammunition. . . . Soldiers and civilians keep asking why the Soviet Union does not send us aid."

Still no help came. And after a month of bitter fighting in May 1942, Tito was forced to make another retreat, this time to the border of Bosnia. In Bosnia, starvation threatened much of the Partisan force.

As the enemy forces prepared to form an airtight ring around him, Tito decided that he must break through and drive toward western Bosnia, where other Partisan troops were in control. This 200-mile campaign, known as the "Long March," took four months but was eventually successfully completed. Along the way the Partisans won a number of engagements and managed to get essential food and ammunition from the defeated enemy units.

This enabled the Partisans to expand the territory over which they maintained control until Tito's forces were poised on the boundary of Croatia. Things were going well for the Partisans, and after the capture of the town of Bihać, Tito radioed Stalin that he was setting up a quasi-governmental body.

The news was not happily received in Moscow. Stalin instructed Tito that his ruling committee must have an all-party, antifascist character and should not be considered a government in any way. Stalin was especially concerned that Tito's action not upset the Allies, who considered the royal Yugoslav government in exile in London as the country's legitimate rulers. "Do not make any mention of a republic," Stalin warned Tito.

Tito, however, pressed ahead. On November 26, 1942, he convened the first meeting of the Anti-Fascist Council of Yugoslavia (AVNOJ), which elected a National Liberation Executive Committee to determine its direction and policies. In a hall hung with Bosnian carpets, hand-drawn portraits of the Allied leaders — England's Prime Minister Winston Churchill, U.S. President Franklin Roosevelt, and Stalin — and home-sewn flags of the Allied countries, Tito set up his committee largely along Stalin's suggested lines. But Tito's own political line was not far below the surface. At a dinner meeting, he answered a toast to his health by saying: "Whatever I have been able to do has been the work of the party. I was young and ignorant and the party took me under its wing and brought me up and trained me. I owe everything to it."

But, as had happened so often before, success for the Partisans was quickly followed by even more strenuous countermeasures from their enemies. Hitler was all too aware of the danger of allowing the Partisans to remain unchecked. As it was, they had tied down a dozen divisions he badly needed on the eastern front against the Soviet Union. He also believed that an Allied invasion of Europe might begin by a landing in Yugoslavia to link up with Tito's forces. Therefore, in January 1943, he launched Op-

The Anti-Fascist Council of Yugoslavia will be the backbone of our struggle; it will organize our devastated country economically and politically.
—JOSIP BROZ TITO
addressing the first session of the council, November 1942

Tito (left) stands with comrade-in-arms Moša Pijade in 1942. Pijade was part of a tightly-knit group of YCP members who had joined Tito in clandestine activities before the war and who would hold key positions in his communist government after hostilities ended. Their shared experiences and backgrounds gave them the solidarity needed to survive the desperate struggle against the Nazis.

In the freezing cold, in shacks or under the open sky, in the woods beside a fire, you can see peasants and their wives; but they do not bewail their fate—they say: 'Dear brothers, fight! We are prepared to give our last crust if it will help you to defeat our common enemy.'
—JOSIP BROZ TITO
speaking to the
first session of the
Anti-Fascist Council
of Yugoslavia (AVNOJ),
November 26, 1942

eration White.

It was during Operation White that Tito scored the dramatic victory in which he escaped encirclement by crossing the Neretva River and defeating the Četniks. Immediately afterward, he faced yet another assault from the Germans. This time, for "Operation Black," the Germans had gathered a total of 100,000 German, Italian, Bulgarian, and Croatian troops against 20,000 of Tito's Partisans. Knowing that the Partisans depended heavily on civilian support, the German commander issued a proclamation: "If the local inhabitants are hostile, treat them with the utmost brutality. If friendly, harness them in the struggle. . . . Destroy anything that could be the slightest use. . . . Foul all water supplies."

Once again the Partisans faced the task of having to break out through the German ring. In bitter fighting, the Partisans pushed north toward Bosnia again. Eventually they found their way barred by a steep river valley with nearly vertical cliffs. The only passage across the valley was a rope bridge, and on the far side the Germans had already assembled a strong line of defense. The German commander was sure that finally he had run his quarry to ground.

"Now that the ring is completely closed," he ordered his men, "you will ensure that no able-bodied man leaves the ring alive."

But Tito was not done yet. He had his soldiers bury all their heavy equipment. All surplus horses were killed and eaten. Despite their exhausted condition and the strength of the enemy attack, the Partisans managed to break through the German encirclement. Tito's men — and women — were back in Bosnia. They quickly faded away into the deep forests of the area. The Germans were too tired to follow.

Now Tito changed his tactics. His army was broken up into small groups, each restricted to a small area. He would not give the Germans another chance to finish off his Partisans at one blow. Although Germany still controlled most of Yugoslavia, Tito had won a great victory simply by being able to survive. The United States and Britain knew this and declared that they would recognize Tito, not Mihajlović, as the leader of the Yugoslav resistance to the Germans.

EASTFOTO

These elderly men showed great courage in joining the Partisan ranks. Tito's army was nearly always on the run, nearly always in danger of encirclement, and always short of supplies. At one point, food was so scarce that soldiers were forced to eat the leaves of beech trees and to squeeze juice from the bark to drink.

7

Recognition

Before 1943, people in the West heard little about the Partisans. Yugoslavia was separated from Britain by all of German-occupied Europe. When news did arrive, it was filtered through the London government-in-exile of King Peter. The victories of Mihajlović, the royalist, were the only ones mentioned.

But the Italians and the Germans knew that Tito was their principal enemy. Messages between the Axis powers referred to Tito so frequently that when the British broke the German codes, his activities could no longer be ignored in London. In addition, British liaison officers with the Četniks reported stories of Tito's success outside the channel provided by King Peter's regime.

This was still not enough, however. The British wanted a closer picture. Thus, in May 1943, in the midst of the crucial German Fifth Offensive, four British officers were parachuted into Montenegro to evaluate the Partisan operations. One of the Britons was killed in an artillery attack in which Tito himself was wounded. The surviving officers sent back favorable reports, but this did not seem to increase the supply of aid. Small quantities went to Tito, while large shipments still went to the Četniks.

Churchill now intervened personally. Dissatisfied with the reports at hand and only partly convinced that the Partisan effort was worth supporting, the

> *I wish that we had a dozen Titos in Germany, leaders with such determination and such good nerves, that even though they were forever encircled they would never give in.*
> —HEINRICH HIMMLER
> leader of the Gestapo, the Nazi secret police, and of the SS, an elite group of Nazi soldiers

By July 1943 Tito had made considerable progress. He had successfully repulsed five Nazi offensives and increased the size of his army to 150,000 troops. He had also extended Partisan political influence by forming in November 1942 the Anti-Fascist Council of Yugoslavia (AVNOJ), an interim assembly that assumed responsibility for governing liberated areas.

UPI/BETTMANN NEWSPHOTOS

From left: Soviet leader Joseph Stalin, United States President Franklin D. Roosevelt, and British Prime Minister Winston Churchill. When the Big Three met in Tehran, Iran, in November 1943 to discuss strategy for combating Hitler, they also decided that Tito was Yugoslavia's most effective resistance figure and therefore deserved strong Allied backing.

British prime minister sent Brigadier Fitzroy Maclean, a tall Scot who had already attained wide knowledge of eastern Europe, to compile information on the Partisans. Maclean quickly gathered a definitive picture of Tito, of his good features — generosity, courage, openness in discussions, and patriotism — and his bad features — vanity and a quick temper.

Tito's closest associates were the men who had started with him: Ranković, in charge of party intelligence; Kardelj, Pijade, and Djilas, party theoreticians; Ivo Ribar, a stirring spokesman; Koča Popović and Peko Dapčević, two brilliant generals. They referred to Tito affectionately as "the old man."

In July 1943 the Allies invaded Sicily, launching the Italian campaign that led to the downfall of Benito Mussolini. However, even though Italy surrendered in September, the Allied troops and the Germans would continue their battles in Italy for a year. Tito did take advantage of the removal of Italy from the war by assuming control of the Yugoslav territory Mussolini's men had occupied. In a few months he controlled much of the country.

This was a situation that the Germans could not allow to continue. They estimated Partisan strength at 110,000 and, now more than ever fearing an Allied landing in Yugoslavia, increased their own forces to 200,000, plus 160,000 Bulgarians and Serbian and Croatian collaborators. With these combined forces they launched Operation Thunderbolt, or the Sixth Offensive, against the Partisans. The force of numbers was on the German side, and soon they had regained the former Italian territory and struck toward Bosnia.

About this time Roosevelt, Churchill, and Stalin met in Tehran, the capital of Iran, to discuss their next moves in the war against Hitler. Their principal topic was the opening of a second front in Western Europe. But they did talk about the Yugoslav theater of operations and, deliberately skirting the issue of whether or not the monarchy should be supported, decided to shift their aid shipments from the Četniks to Tito.

To Tito, this was the moment for political action. At the end of November 1943, in the midst of Operation Thunderbolt, in the Bosnian town of Jajce, he called a conference at which the delegates proclaimed the formation of a communist government, called the National Liberation Committee, to replace

Edvard Kardelj (left) and Tito in a cave near the town of Drvar, where the Partisans set up headquarters in early 1944. By then Tito was receiving significant aid from Great Britain and the United States. A few months earlier, at the second gathering of the Anti-Fascist Council, delegates had named Tito marshal of Yugoslavia in a provisional government called the National Liberation Committee.

After a 16-year hiatus, Zarko Broz, Tito's son by his first wife, Pelagea, was reunited with his father in 1944 at the Partisans' new command center on the island of Vis. Zarko is pictured wearing the Order of the Red Star, the Soviet army's highest honor, which he earned near Moscow in 1941.

the monarchy. The gathering also proclaimed Tito marshal of Yugoslavia. For the first time since he had left prison nine years earlier, the Yugoslav leader now went openly by his real name, adorned with his political alias. Thereafter he was known to the world as Marshal Josip Broz Tito.

Stalin complained that the proclamation was "a stab in the back." But Tito had other things to worry about. Once more the Partisans were threatened with encirclement. Germans on skis and in motorized columns drove Tito out of Jajce. Despite the bitter cold of early winter and the loss of supplies, Tito was able to get his detachments to safety in the mountains. By the end of February the German offensive had dwindled. Operation Thunderbolt, like its five predecessors, had failed to capture Tito.

Tito now moved his headquarters out of the mountains to a cave above the town of Drvar. Here he was able to enjoy the fruits of his long campaign for recognition by the Allies. Even the Russians parachuted in liaison officers. Tito contemplated establishing more convenient and spacious quarters.

The Germans had other ideas, however. Just as dawn was breaking one morning late in May, they launched a heavy airborne attack on Tito's cave. Operation Knight's Move had begun. The paratroopers' guns blazed into the mouth of the cave, but Tito and his staff escaped by climbing to the cliff top through a passage behind a waterfall. Even more fortunately, German ground troops involved in the attack were a day late in reaching Drvar, and when they finally arrived, they found their quarry gone.

The British flew Tito to safety first in Italy and then to the island of Vis, off the Yugoslav coast, in an area that the Partisans controlled with British help. There Tito was reunited with his son Zarko, whom he had last seen as a boy. The handsome young man looked remarkably like his father at a similar age, though he had already lost an arm in the war.

Churchill, meanwhile, announced that Britain would cease supplying the Četniks, stating simply that Mihajlović "has not been fighting the enemy, and moreover some of his subordinates have been making accommodations with the enemy."

Churchill thus removed the last barrier to recognition of the communist revolutionary Tito. But Tito had made some compromises, too. On June 16, 1944, he agreed with royalist representative Dr. Ivan Šubašić to the tentative formation of a provisional government in which the communists and monarchists would share power and in which Mihajlović would play no part. Despite the resolution by the Jajce conference insisting that King Peter would not be permitted to return to Yugoslavia because he had fled in wartime, Tito agreed that the fate of the monarchy would be deferred until a postwar plebiscite, or popular vote, determined its future.

Tito accordingly was given full recognition as an Allied commander. In late summer 1944 he held two important meetings. The first, in Italy, was with Churchill. Despite continued differences of opinion over the Yugoslav monarchy and the person of King Peter, the two strong men got on famously, so much so that Churchill voiced regret that he was too old

> *The vast majority of the Yugoslav people came to recognize, while the war was still in progress, that it was necessary to create a new and better social system. That is why it was possible while the war was still in progress to forge unity among the working classes, the predominant section of the poor and medium peasantry, and the people's intelligentsia . . . building socialism in the country.*
> —JOSIP BROZ TITO

to parachute into Yugoslavia to see Tito's forces in action.

The next meeting was quite different. Tito flew secretly to Moscow to confer with Stalin. The relaxed atmosphere of the meeting with Churchill was replaced by coolness and touchiness. Stalin advised Tito that he expected the Partisans to obey Russian commanders when the Soviet forces reached Yugoslavia. Tito replied that his men took orders from no one but him, and he followed up by presenting Stalin with a list of permissible Soviet military actions in his country. Moreover, he stressed that there could be no political activity of any kind by the Russian forces. Stalin's suggestion that some centrist Yugoslav politicians could be trusted in a postwar coalition government was rejected.

On Tito's return, he found the Germans pulling back northward through Yugoslavia. In pursuit, the

Tito with Peko Dapčević, center, and Koča Popović, right. These two were considered the Partisans' most brilliant commanders. By the fall of 1944, Partisan forces under their control were poised for the liberation of Belgrade.

Red Army crossed into Yugoslavia from Romania. Bulgaria switched to the Allied side in the conflict. The German position was crumbling rapidly, enabling Tito's top generals, Dapčević and Popović, with Soviet ground support and air cover provided by the Americans, to converge on Belgrade. But there the Germans dug in. Now the battle had to be fought block by block and house by house.

On October 20, 1944, after a week of heavy fighting in which the Germans lost 16,000 dead and 8,000 taken prisoner, the last stronghold in Belgrade, the old Turkish citadel, fell to the First Proletarian Brigade, and the remaining Germans fled. As the Germans retreated, their Serbian, Četnik, and Ustaša supporters fled with them. The Germans kept a foothold in northern Croatia during the winter, but gradually they were forced out entirely.

In early 1945 Tito resumed negotiations with Šubašić to modify the provisional government, which had been agreed to in June 1944 but still had not been put into effect. It was agreed that Tito's Anti-Fascist Council would be the supreme legislative body, while the executive would combine representatives of the royal government and the YCP — with Tito as prime minister and Šubašić as foreign secretary. The settlement was submitted to and approved by Great Britain and the Soviet Union, both of which soon thereafter sent ambassadors to Belgrade. Tito openly admitted that he had accepted the Šubašić pact only to mollify the Western powers, whose aid he needed desperately. By this time he was much more powerful than the royalists. His troops controlled most of Yugoslavia's territory. He had installed civil authorities in local governments with party members in key positions. During 1944, while negotiations on the provisional government continued, his National Liberation Committee had ruled as a government.

On May 7, 1945, Germany surrendered. The war in Europe was over. Some of the Germans had held out to the end. In Zagreb, Pavelić told a group of Ustaša women that they should do the same and die like heroes. He then fled to South America, by way of Austria. Mihajlović hid out in the mountains.

Let us not be too carried away by our successes in the battlefield, but rather think of how we are going to build our towns, our railways, our roads, our villages, and fields, so that the coming generation will be able to say that their fathers did everything they could to leave them a better inheritance.
—JOSIP BROZ TITO
speaking to a crowd in Belgrade, March 27, 1945

8

The People's Republic

After years of indescribable hardship and privation, of constant danger and struggle, Josip Broz Tito, marshal of Yugoslavia, had emerged triumphant. His miraculous military victories, attained against extraordinary odds, had earned him international renown and the adoration of his countrymen — along with immense political power. Under the compromise agreement with the royalist faction, Tito was prime minister of the reunited nation. But now, in the summer of 1945, he wished to extend Partisan power to bring about his true goal: the establishment of a communist state. His efforts in this direction were enhanced by two factors. The wartime emplacement of Partisan organizations in liberated areas gave him control over most local governments. In addition, he was immensely popular. Most Yugoslavians considered Tito's leadership of a postwar government to be the natural course of action. Support for the monarchy had all but disappeared when the king fled the Nazi invasion and refused, from his safe haven in England, to aid resistance movements. By 1945 prewar political arrangements seemed, in the words of historian Phyllis Auty, "outdated and irrelevant; politicians who had spent the war years abroad were discredited . . . since they had not shared the nation's transforming and cathartic experiences." Ultimately, there was little resistance when, in the summer of 1945, Tito subverted the Šubašić agreement

> *There are villages that have been burned a dozen times over during the war. But on the other hand, what strength emanates from the people? On all sides, the people ask for nails, for lumber; they are patching houses and schools the best they can.*
> —JOSIP BROZ TITO
> speaking in 1945

Following the war, it was accepted as a given by most Yugoslavians that Tito would become the next leader of their nation. Buoyed by his tremendous popularity and his broad network of Partisan political organizations, Tito reneged on his promise to share power, easily eliminated the monarchists, and set up a communist state.

and took sole control of the national government by eliminating the monarchists. Pending reorganization of the government, day-to-day affairs continued to be managed by a war council, in which Tito had the final say. Meeting in Moscow in 1944, Churchill and Stalin had agreed that after the war their nations would share control of the Balkan state. But by mid-1945 the country belonged to Marshal Tito.

Though Tito clearly enjoyed widespread support, he maintained strict control over the country until plans could be made for an election to validate his regime. He had worked too hard for his revolution to allow internal opposition or outside interference to prevent its completion. A Partisan intelligence agency, developed during the war by Tito's aide Aleksander Ranković, rounded up known collaborators and tried and executed many of them. Members of the Yugoslavian aristocracy who had not openly supported the Partisans during the war were intimidated or imprisoned. Heavily armed Partisan soldiers guarded every government office and aggressively patrolled the streets of every town and village.

As leader, the man who had spent much of his childhood hungry, who as a young adult had walked half of Europe in search of employment, did not

Soviet troops parade through Belgrade after joining with the Partisans to liberate the Yugoslavian capital in 1944. For years thereafter, Tito was happily ensconced in a villa on the outskirts of the city, where he indulged in pleasures that were unavailable to him during his impoverished childhood.

TASS FROM SOVFOTO

hesitate to enjoy the fruits of his labor. Following the liberation of Belgrade, Tito, his wife, Herta, and a staff of volunteer servants had taken over a suburban walled villa. There Tito and his comrades enjoyed meals fit for kings: gourmet meats, fine wines served in large gold goblets, the best Turkish coffees. A team of tailors was hired to create a wardrobe worthy of a distinguished statesman. For entertainment, he had a stable of thoroughbred horses, a speedboat, a yacht, and a fleet of expensive automobiles. Cutting a dashing figure in finely cut military uniforms, he frequently hosted lavish receptions for foreign dignitaries at the refurbished palace of Prince Paul. He thrived in his new role as diplomat, charming visitors with his friendly wit. According to one frequently told story, he entertained guests at a dinner party in his honor at the American ambassador's residence by pretending to be the butler. When the phone rang, he screamed at an unsuspecting caller, "Don't you know better than to disturb the American ambassador when he is entertaining the great Marshal Tito?"

Tito's opulent lifestyle did not hinder his tireless pursuit of a burning dream: "to found a state that was new not only in form but in content as well . . . a socialist state." Tito hoped to establish an economy based on the ideas of Karl Marx, an economy in which the means of production — that is, factories, farms, retail businesses — would in theory be given to the proletariat, or working classes, thereby eliminating worker exploitation. Since Tito sought to imitate the Soviet model, industry would in fact be closely controlled by the state, which in turn would be controlled by the party, specifically by a small, elite group of high-ranking party officials known as the politburo. Such a system would be protected from dissent by a secret police — a climate of fear being necessary to safeguard the revolution and to guarantee its benefits: an improved standard of living, an end to the alienation of workers from their labor, and an end to inequality of opportunity.

Tito was faced with rebuilding a nation that lay in charred ruins. The Nazis had laid waste to the countryside, burning thousands of villages, blowing

Yugoslav children orphaned by World War II. The war left wounds that would perhaps never heal — entire villages had been wiped out, roads ripped up, bridges blown apart, factories destroyed. Approximately 2 million Yugoslavs died in the conflict. Economic damage was estimated at $61 billion.

up hundreds of roads, and wiping out most of Yugoslavia's bridges. Economic damage was estimated at $61 billion: a third of the nation's factories, half of its railroad tracks, half of its coal mines were lost. One out of every nine Yugoslavians — 2 million people — had died in the conflict and almost twice as many had been wounded. Tito managed to secure some aid from UNRRA, a UN relief agency, but there were restrictions on how the money could be used, since the United States, the program's primary contributor, was suspicious of Tito's communist orientation.

Locating additional sources of economic aid and protecting Yugoslavia's position in a seemingly hostile Western world became the primary goals of the new regime's foreign policy. Though the top leadership of the YCP made decisions on domestic policy in a collegial fashion, Tito exerted special influence over the sphere of foreign affairs. His congenial personality and adeptness at negotiating made him a remarkably effective diplomat.

Most relief aid came from the Soviet Union, with whom Yugoslavia established its strongest foreign ties. Despite the Soviet Union's miserly withholding of support during the war, a close relationship was almost inevitable. The formation of the YCP in 1920 had been inspired by the Soviet state, and the YCP had thereafter looked continually to Stalin's country for ideological guidance and technical training. As Tito explained in later years, "We had great confidence in the Soviet Union until 1947, and the Russians had a great deal of influence on the organization of our state, because we took them as our example." In 1945 the two countries signed the Treaty of Friendship and Mutual Assistance, after which, on Yugoslav request, the Soviet Union sent hundreds of military, economic, and cultural advisers to Belgrade.

There were, however, minor squabbles that presaged future conflict. One developed over the wanton behavior of Red Army soldiers following the liberation of Belgrade. Milovan Djilas complained to the Soviets after the war that their soldiers had looted shops, raped Yugoslavian women, and dam-

With Stalin (second from right) and Soviet Foreign Minister Vyacheslav Molotov (far right) looking on, Tito signs the Treaty of Friendship and Mutual Assistance in April 1945. After the treaty was concluded, the Soviet Union sent hundreds of advisers to Belgrade in an attempt to control Yugoslavia's army, economy, and cultural life.

SOVFOTO

aged a lot of property. The excitable Stalin did not take kindly to these accusations of "unworthy behavior." Trouble also arose over attempts by the Soviet secret police to recruit Yugoslav citizens. These efforts, however, most often proved futile.

These minor disputes with the Soviets were overshadowed, however, by the deterioration of relations with the West. Allied generosity and extensive military cooperation had resulted in a strong friendship during the waning stages of World War II, but even before the war had ended, the Trieste Crisis of May 1945 had broken this bond apart. As British and Partisan troops combined to push the Germans out of northern Italy in April 1945, Tito told British leaders that after the war he planned to claim Trieste and its hinterlands. Trieste was a port city on the Adriatic Sea that Italy had held since the collapse of the Austro-Hungarian Empire in World War I but that had been heavily settled by Slovenes. Churchill responded that he preferred to settle Trieste's future at postwar peace conferences. Tito took matters into his own hands, sending Partisan troops to occupy the area and formally announcing plans to annex the area on May 1. On May 3, after Tito made his intentions known, fresh Allied soldiers streamed into the city and took up positions only blocks from the Yugoslavs. Tito ordered his commanders, "Retain the town at all costs. Beware of provocations, but stand firm." Nerves frayed under the intense pressure; sporadic exchanges of gunfire broke out; on one occasion, British pursuit planes strafed the Yugoslavian occupation zone. U.S. President Harry S. Truman confided to his advisers that he feared the crisis might spark World War III.

Stalin at first appeared to sanction Tito's action, saying, "It would be an undeserved insult to refuse Yugoslavia the right to occupy the territory retaken from the enemy after the Yugoslav people have made so many sacrifices." But, worried that the conflict might damage his own relations with the British and hence jeopardize his plans to control Eastern Europe, Stalin clandestinely promised the British that he would remain uninvolved. Left alone to face the strongest powers in the world, Tito quickly

Tito addresses a crowd of 250,000 supporters during the Trieste Crisis. The Yugoslav leader's attempt to annex Trieste in May 1945 started a downward spiral in Yugoslavia's relations with the West. Though ultimately Tito relinquished his claim to the former Italian city, he gained the support of many noncommunist Yugoslavs with his strong nationalistic stand during the crisis.

agreed to a compromise. But he remained bitter about being used as a pawn in the growing Cold War game, saying on May 27, "We demand that everyone shall be master in his own house. We do not want to pay for others; we do not want to be used as a bribe in international bargaining. We do not want to become involved in any policy primarily concerned with spheres of interest." His comments revealed his strong will and his thirst for independence and foreshadowed his later refusal to join either the Soviet or the U.S. camp. His nationalistic message disturbed Soviet leaders, who expected younger communist nations to be deferential toward their country.

Meanwhile, Stalin was busy consolidating Soviet political control over the Eastern European countries that Red Army troops had occupied during the final months of World War II. Stalin had promised Churchill and Roosevelt at the Yalta Conference of February 1945 that he would hold free elections in these nations, but after the war governments loyal to Moscow were established in Poland, Czechoslovakia, Hungary, Romania, Bulgaria, Albania, and

As the first step in creating a communist political system, Tito formed the Constituent Assembly in November 1945. The parliamentary body had no real power, serving merely to validate automatically decisions made by the Communist party's highest body, the politburo, which consisted of Tito and his closest advisers.

East Germany. Stalin proceeded to remodel each nation's political institutions, economic system, and social arrangements along Soviet lines. The puppet communist regimes were kept loyal with attractive trade agreements, military aid, diplomatic pacts, and constant observation by Soviet secret police. In typical Stalinesque terms, they were portrayed officially as "people's democracies." In 1946 Churchill described these Soviet efforts to secure its western frontier as an "iron curtain" falling over Eastern Europe.

Against this background, American leaders naturally feared that Yugoslavia would become yet another Soviet satellite. Suspicions grew as American diplomats stationed in Belgrade after the war sent home reports of widespread political terror and inequitable distribution of UNRRA relief. "If you are a Partisan, you eat; if you are not, you starve," one official said. For his part, Tito fumed over rumors that Britain was planning a military invasion to restore the monarchy. He was also annoyed by the disparity between the quantity of Western aid given to his country and that given to West Germany. "You give more aid and goodwill to a defeated Germany — the common enemy who invaded Yugoslavia — than us, their victim," he told U.S. Ambassador Richard C. Patterson.

Western leaders were further alienated when, in autumn 1945, Tito abandoned his promise to consult Yugoslav citizens on how to replace the monarchy and exchanged the provisional government for a permanent, Soviet-style political apparatus. Tito felt no remorse about ignoring the agreement, claiming it had been forced upon him by "stubborn Western powers." When on November 11, 1945, elections were held for Yugoslavia's new parliamentary body, the Constituent Assembly, Šubašić and the royal opposition were prohibited from registering candidates. (Shortly thereafter the royalist leaders resigned their posts and were placed under house arrest.) In the election, voters were asked to vote for or against a single slate of candidates: 470 YCP members and 40 nonmembers running for 510 seats. The United States was disappointed with

Tito addresses the Constituent Assembly in 1945. In the first elections for the parliamentary body, only one nominee, usually a Communist, was on the ballot for each seat. The assembly's first act formally abolished the monarchy and made Yugoslavia a federal people's republic.

what was seen as a violation of democratic procedure. Tito went to great lengths to ensure a large turnout and a strong show of support — even manning the polls with heavily armed troops — but most analysts agreed he would have won a majority in a free election.

The elections were central to Tito's consolidation of power, giving him a legal mandate to rule. But the Constituent Assembly, like the Soviet parliament, was a powerless body, prohibited from undertaking any independent legislative action. It existed merely to provide a semblance of democratic procedure, automatically ratifying decisions made elsewhere. Real power continued to reside in the Communist party. In Tito's new government, the YCP retained the structure it had borrowed before the war from the Soviet Union. In theory, the supreme organ of the party was the party congress, but these gatherings convened only once every few years for about 10 days. In the interim, decisions were made by the small political bureau, or politburo, and endorsed by the larger central committee of the Communist party. The politburo, the inner circle of communists who had run the party since before the war, consisted of Tito, Edvard Kardelj, Moša Pijade, Aleksander Ranković, and Milovan Djilas. Each became responsible for a particular field: Kardelj for day-to-day foreign policy; Pijade for legal matters and Marxist theory; Ranković for the security apparatus; and Djilas for literary and propaganda work. Tito himself, as prime minister, held a special position. He was the top representative to foreign leaders, he coordinated the work of the rest of his team, and he had final say in all matters. Politburo meetings were held several times a week, and lively discussions often produced disagreements, but once a decision had been made, opposition had to be abandoned.

On November 29, 1945, the Constituent Assembly passed its first measure, officially abolishing the monarchy and establishing the Federal People's Republic of Yugoslavia, composed of six republics: Serbia, Croatia, Slovenia, Bosnia-Hercegovina, Macedonia, and Montenegro. Once the new feder-

ated structure was in place, Tito instituted a series of laws designed to foster national unity while at the same time guaranteeing regional autonomy and ethnic diversity. Discrimination against minorities was outlawed, republics were given the right to determine their own official languages, and ethnic groups were given the option of having separate educational systems and mass media. The government was also to promote cultural and educational exchange programs among nationalities and to encourage workers to seek employment outside their republic of origin.

At the same time, Tito began to reorganize the economy. The state appropriated without compensation, and took over management of, most private industry, including banks, businesses, and factories. Only craftsmen working without hired labor were allowed to remain independent of the vast state-controlled economic apparatus. Ownership of homes was restricted to one dwelling, and renting of private property was prohibited. Yugoslavians

Tito surrounded by members of a workers' collective. In 1946, following Stalin's example, Tito began to collectivize agriculture and launched an ambitious — some said too ambitious — Five-Year Plan aimed at increasing industrial production. Stalin was concerned by Tito's attempt to make Yugoslavia economically self-sufficient.

were permitted to own land, but holdings were limited to 60 acres. Under the Agrarian Reform Law of 1945, the government confiscated agricultural properties in excess of 60 acres and estates owned by banks, companies, monasteries, absentee landlords, and collaborators. The vacant land was distributed among landless peasants, who were then required to join collective farms.

Tito's extensive economic and political changes would eventually be incorporated into a constitution developed in 1946 and passed into law on January 31, 1947. That constitution would also grant on paper many rights that in fact were not allowed in postwar Yugoslavia — freedom of the press, of association, of assembly. In fact, the new Yugoslavia was quite undemocratic. Tito and his comrades were legitimately interested in improving the quality of life in Yugoslavia. But, convinced that their program for reform was the only enlightened one, they refused to tolerate dissent.

In November 1946 Tito launched the first Five-Year Plan, a massive campaign to industrialize Yugoslavia and to make it economically self-sufficient. The program was meticulously charted, with yearly, monthly, and daily schedules drawn up for each republic, each industry, each factory. The plan was so extensive that the paper on which it was printed was said to weigh 3,300 pounds. Tito hoped to increase industrial production and the size of the proletariat, which, according to Marxist theory, was to form the backbone of a communist country and which, in practice, would expand the ranks of the YCP. Planners projected large increases in the standard of living, in the employment rate, and in the availability of consumer goods.

The ambitiousness of the mobilization reflected the indefatigably optimistic spirit of the Partisans, who had succeeded during World War II mostly because of gritty determination. This time, however, desire was not enough. Because of improper management, many basic consumer items like combs and sewing needles were left out of the plan and hence became scarce, while other goods were produced too generously and ended up stored in warehouses. Not enough funds were available to finance construction of factories, and because of the emphasis on quantity of production, the quality of goods suffered.

At the same time, the country experienced an agricultural crisis. Landowning peasants chafed under government price controls and demands to step up production. Though Tito threatened fines and imprisonment, peasants refused to produce more food than was needed by their families, causing an acute food shortage. The situation was exacerbated by an ill-fated campaign to force peasants onto collective farms, which was seen as a way of giving the state ownership of the land and control of production. Tito's plan met the same resistance Stalin's had during the 1930s.

Yugoslavia's postwar poverty was so extreme that the average Yugoslav had to work five weeks to earn enough money to buy a pair of shoes. Most citizens had to hold two jobs just to make ends meet. Murmurs of discontent were heard. But Tito persisted with his program of economic change, convinced that the situation demanded drastic action.

Soviet leaders were deeply disturbed by Tito's decision to industrialize, fearing that it would lead to greater political independence for Yugoslavia and the loss of a valuable source of raw materials for the Soviet Union. Traditionally, Yugoslavia's primary economic strength had been in natural resources, such as bauxite, zinc, and chromium. These minerals — which could be processed and refined into aluminum, steel, and other marketable metals — were mined in the southern provinces for export to foreign factories, primarily in the Soviet Union. One of Tito's first acts as the Yugoslav leader was to nationalize the mines and begin construction of processing plants. Stalin's response was short and to the point: "What do you want with a heavy industry? We have everything you need in the Urals." Tito's decision to go his own way was an agonizing one, but industrialization was an essential step in the formative process of a communist nation. He was beginning to realize that the Soviet Union's interests were not necessarily those of Yugoslavia.

We did not wish to halt halfway: to depose the king and abolish the monarchy and to come to power only to share it with representatives of the capitalist class, who would continue to exploit the working masses of Yugoslavia.
—JOSIP BROZ TITO explaining in 1946 his drastic reorganization of the Yugoslav economy

I had against me a rival organization, the Communist party, which sought its aims without compromise. . . . I was surrounded by every imaginable intelligence service, British, American, Russian, and German. I wanted much, I began much, but the gale of the world carried me and my work away.

—DRAŽA MIHAJLOVIĆ
at his trial by a Communist
court, June–July 1946

Yugoslavia did continue to imitate the Soviet model in its intolerance of political opposition. Aleksander Ranković's secret police became ruthlessly efficient, going so far as to index all Yugoslavian citizens with loyalty ratings ranging from "trustworthy" to "dangerous." Tito gave Ranković free reign to deal summarily with suspected enemies of the Communist party.

His first target was Draža Mihajlović. At the end of the war, Mihajlović had remained at large, roaming the mountains on the border between Bosnia and Serbia, aided only by a few loyal soldiers. Though he had lost his wireless radio and was cut off from supporters outside the country, he remained in Yugoslavia, convinced that he would someday lead a Serbian nationalist uprising that would overthrow the communist regime. By 1946 all of his men had been killed or captured or had deserted. He lived in a trench by day and crawled into small towns only under the safe cover of nightfall. Bedraggled and fatigued, he was finally captured in March by the secret police and charged with high treason, collaboration with the enemy, and numerous war crimes.

Tito insisted that Mihajlović be brought to trial — rather than quietly disposed of — in order to present to the international community all the facts about the Četnik leader's wartime activities. Mihajlović's highly publicized trial, which began on June 10, 1946, and lasted more than a month, also became a forum for propagandistic attacks by the Yugoslavian government on the United States and Great Britain, who were accused of abetting Mihajlović in his campaign against the communists. Dressed in his old uniform, the former minister of war for the Yugoslav monarchy presented his own defense, denying all charges. In a courageous and poignant final speech, he gave a detailed account of his involvement in the war and of "the whirlpool of events" in which he had been caught. Along with other Četniks, he was executed on July 17, 1946.

Next Tito turned his attention to the head of the Catholic hierarchy in Croatia, Bishop Aloysius Stepinac, who was arrested and brought to trial in September 1946. Stepinac was charged with various forms of collaboration: publicly blessing the Nazi army, as shown in captured newsreels; forcing Partisan prisoners to choose between death by the Ustaša or conversion; and sitting in the Ustaša parliament in the Croatian puppet state during the war. In his defense, Stepinac claimed collaboration helped to mitigate the harsh actions of the Nazis. Most historians concur that Stepinac had in fact gradually become disgusted by Pavelić's reign of terror. But he had clearly been profascist, and he was ultimately convicted as an "enemy of the people" and sentenced to 16 years of hard labor.

The arrest of the Catholic bishop was part of Tito's crusade to undermine church power and popularity, an effort motivated more by a fear of a powerful rival than by doctrinaire Marxist atheism. During the first two years of his regime, Tito confiscated over 160,000 acres of church lands in Croatia, Serbia, and Slovenia. Stepinac claimed during his trial that the communists had killed 260 to 270 priests, telling Tito, "The people will never forgive you for that." The Serbian Orthodox church, which openly opposed communism — calling for compulsory religious education and its own establishment as the state religion — received especially harsh treatment. Tito confiscated 90 percent of its land under the Agrarian Reform Law and converted many of its elegant cathedrals and monasteries into public museums, workers' vacation resorts, and hospitals.

Tito's treatment of the church further strained relations with the West. In the United States, conservative congressmen called for action against Yugoslavia amid a rising tide of anticommunism.

In the meantime, American reconnaissance planes teased Yugoslavian air defenses with constant overflights, zipping over — despite Tito's protests — from bases in Austria and Italy. Then on August 9, 1946, an American transport plane was fired on by Yugoslav fighter jets and forced to the ground in Yugoslavia, where its nine passengers were arrested. Ten days later, another American transport was shot down, and five crew members died in a fiery crash. Americans were furious. The

Speaking before a Belgrade crowd in August 1946, Tito defends his nation's actions in shooting down two unarmed American transport planes as a legitimate protection of Yugoslavia's sovereignty. His country wanted peace, he said, "but not peace at any price."

U.S. State Department demanded release of the survivors and reparations for the lost planes. Eventually, Tito offered a tepid apology and set free the American fliers, but the affair produced a bitterness that took a long time to dissipate.

To Western leaders, acrimonious relations with Tito were proof that Yugoslavia had become a Soviet colony in the Balkans. In truth, a large rift was opening between the two nations. While Yugoslavia defied Stalin by forging ahead with its ambitious program for industrialization, the swarm of Soviet advisers in Belgrade continued to offend Partisan pride. The rift reflected deep-seated differences. Because of their long tradition of self-reliance, especially during the solitary wartime struggle, the Partisans were reluctant to forfeit power to any outside group, even the Soviet Union. To Tito, preserving his country's political independence was essential to ensure that Yugoslavia could modify socialism in accordance with its own historic traditions and sociocultural conditions. The Yugoslav communists differed from their Soviet counterparts, in the view of historian Wolfgang Leonhard, "by a far greater understanding, by a much more marked international approach to problems and by sounder Marxist knowledge than was to be found among the dogmatic and bureaucratic — and frequently nationalistic — representatives of Moscow." Stalin thought that the Soviet Union's historical position as the founder of communism, along with its enormous military and economic strength, granted it unquestioned leadership of younger communist nations.

Stalin fumed as Tito pursued an increasingly activist foreign policy. Dressed in his finest military uniforms, Tito made a grand tour of Eastern Europe in 1946 and 1947 and was given a hero's welcome in every capital. During these visits, he discussed mutual problems with his fellow communist leaders and concluded bilateral agreements — without consulting Moscow. He formed a customs union with Albania and signed defense pacts with Poland, Czechoslovakia, and Hungary. Stalin was also disturbed by Tito's support of communists rebelling against the government of Greece. At the end of the war, Stalin had agreed to leave Greece in Great Britain's sphere of influence. Tito's actions, seen by the British as Soviet engineered, threatened Stalin's agenda for Eastern Europe.

Attempting to establish stricter control over Yugoslavia and other Eastern European nations, Stalin formed the Cominform, the Communist Information Bureau, in September 1947. The Cominform's stated function was to coordinate the exchange of information between communist parties and to establish a unified approach to policy — "on a basis of mutual agreement." But by setting up the Cominform's headquarters in Belgrade, Stalin hoped to use the agency to collect intelligence information on the Yugoslavs and to drive a wedge between Yugoslavia and the other states in the Cominform.

Tito continued to flout Soviet authority. He proposed the creation of a Balkan federation to Bulgarian leaders — again without consulting Moscow. Then he issued a fierce critique of the policies of many Cominform countries, assuming a role that Stalin had always reserved for himself: oracle of Marxist orthodoxy. Stalin could no longer sit idly, watching his disciple betray him. Tito's deviations from the "party line" were doing serious damage to Soviet prestige. Stalin considered the betrayal especially heinous because, to his mind, the Red Army had freed Belgrade from the Nazis and thus had been responsible for the establishment of the Partisan regime. He had to act — either by forcing Tito to apologize and change his direction or by removing Tito from power. Tito was up against a man who had once said, "There's nothing sweeter than to bide the proper moment for revenge, to insert the knife, twist it, and then go home for a good night's sleep."

> *Tito showed qualities of statesmanship that gave Yugoslavia prestige such as it has never had since its foundation as a state, and won for himself respect and—sometimes reluctant—admiration throughout the world.*
> —PHYLLIS AUTY
> British historian

9

Break with Moscow

The year 1948 opened on an ominous note for Tito, as Stalin summoned him to the Kremlin. Tito chose to send Edvard Kardelj and Milovan Djilas in his place, but even before they left Belgrade, further troubles developed. Tito's treatment of the Russian ambassador — who was provided the same amenities and courtesies as all other diplomats in Belgrade — provoked the ire of Soviet Foreign Minister Vyacheslav Molotov. Molotov sent a stinging note to Tito that said, among other things, "In a truly communist nation, the Russian ambassador is certainly entitled to expect a special status above that of ordinary diplomats from bourgeois governments." The nations also collided over Tito's unilateral decision to provide military support to Albania in its border war with Greece. This time the written rebuke came from Stalin himself. Tito was told that if he did not immediately cancel the agreement with Albania, the Yugoslavs would be publicly denounced.

When the Kremlin meeting was finally held, on February 10, it was obvious that the Soviets had decided to take a harder line. Molotov opened the conference with an acerbic speech that alluded darkly to the presence of "serious differences" between Moscow and Belgrade. Later, Stalin upbraided Kardelj for Yugoslavia's backing of the Greek communists. Finally, Stalin proposed the di-

Stalin envisaged us as being his satellites after the war. We did not even think of it as a possibility.
—JOSIP BROZ TITO

By 1948 Tito's activist foreign policy and his decision to industrialize against Moscow's wishes had whipped Joseph Stalin into a fury. The Soviet leader was determined to force Tito to abandon his independent course. "I will shake my little finger and there will be no more Tito," Stalin threatened.

THE BETTMANN ARCHIVE

Vyacheslav Molotov, the Soviet foreign minister and Stalin's right-hand man, played a key role in applying political pressure to Tito in 1948. In March he coauthored, with Stalin, a threatening letter to Tito comparing the Yugoslav marshal with two discredited anti-Stalinists, Leon Trotsky and Nikolai Bukharin.

vision of Eastern Europe into three federations: Hungary and Romania; Poland and Czechoslovakia; Yugoslavia and Bulgaria. Though Tito himself had earlier suggested similar federations, the Soviet proposal was judged by Kardelj and his comrades to be a trick by which Stalin hoped to gain greater control of Yugoslavia. They left Moscow having signed only an agreement for mutual consultation.

Along with direct pressure on Yugoslav communists, Stalin organized a "whispering campaign" to discredit Tito in Cominform countries. Dutiful communists passed along the message "There is something wrong with Yugoslavia." As spring arrived, Tito's portraits began disappearing from Eastern Europe, tourist travel to Yugoslavia slowed, and Yugoslavia's invitation to the Leipzig Spring Fair was withdrawn. Soviet-Yugoslav trade slowed considerably after the Soviet Ministry of Foreign Trade broke off negotiations for a new exchange agreement. Finally, after Tito insisted that he could no longer pay the high salaries of Soviet advisers and rebuffed attempts to subordinate Ranković's secret police to the Soviet secret police, the NKVD, Stalin withdrew the Soviet military and civilian advisers from Belgrade.

The conflict resumed toward the end of March, in a series of confidential letters. Tito wrote the first, telling Molotov that he was "surprised and hurt" by the recall of advisers and imploring him to reveal the "real reason" for the Kremlin order. On March 27 Tito received an eight-page, single-spaced profusion of Stalinist invective. It castigated the leaders of the YCP as ideologically unsound, ignorant of the views of their rank and file, and guilty of harboring British spies. The most disarming section of the letter likened Tito to Trotsky and Nikolai Bukharin (one of Stalin's former rivals), a threat that — in view of Trotsky's assassination by an NKVD agent and Bukharin's execution — was not to be misunderstood. Tito was at first taken aback: "I felt as if a thunderbolt had struck me." He realized that he had reached a critical juncture. To apologize or recant now would mean permanent renunciation of political independence, while to respond in kind would be tantamount to a declaration of war.

Tito spent days fretting over his response. After conferring with Djilas, Kardelj, and Ranković, he submitted his resignation. The group rejected the offer out of hand.

Meanwhile, Stalin circulated copies of his diatribe against Tito to East European leaders, who quickly seconded the charges. Stalin was sure he could conquer Tito by dividing the YCP, whose members, he sensed, feared the ideological confusion and economic difficulty that would result from a complete break in relations. "I will shake my little finger and there will be no more Tito," Stalin told Soviet politburo member Nikita Khrushchev.

At this crucial time, Tito turned to his wellspring of constant support, those who had been with him in the darkest days of the war — the central core of the Communist party. He arranged a meeting of the central committee of the YCP, to be held on April 12, 1948. As members filed into the library of the Alexander Palace at Dedinje, on the outskirts of Belgrade, the mood was tense: not only was Tito's whole career in jeopardy, but the future of Yugoslavia hung in the balance. One of the first speakers, Sretan "Black" Žujović, attacked Tito's actions: "I am against such an attitude. How can we convince ourselves and the people that we are on the right path if the Soviet party and Stalin do not approve?" Tito's response was incisive: "This is not a matter of theoretical discussion or ideological error. The issue at stake is the relationship between one country and another." One by one each member — except Žujović — rose to agree with Tito. They also voted to send a letter that included what has become known as the motto of Tito's movement: "No matter how much each of us loves the land of socialism, the USSR, he can, in no case, love his own country less." The meeting had been a major turning point. It was the first time an entire communist party had stood up to the Soviet Union. Moreover, Tito was assured that he could depend thereafter on the loyalty of the party leadership.

Having failed to sow dissension among Yugoslavia's leaders, Stalin shifted the focus of his cam-

> *We're a mad bunch, we Yugoslavs. We're only at our best when any big power tries to bully our little country— whether it's Germany invading us, America violating our air space, or the Soviet Union trying to force us to our knees.*
> —MILOVAN DJILAS
> member of the
> Yugoslav politburo

paign toward driving a wedge between the party leadership and its following and isolating Yugoslavia in the international community. At Stalin's urging, Soviet satellite countries let loose a barrage of propaganda, denouncing Tito as a fascist, a murderer, a British secret service agent, an insolent dwarf, and a "troubadour of Wall Street." Soviet agents were sent into Yugoslavia to stir up trouble.

For their part, the Yugoslav leaders calmly and systematically refuted the charges made against them. They argued that love of the Soviet Union had been "stubbornly inculcated into the masses of the YCP and the people in general." They disputed claims that Yugoslavia clung to aspects of capitalism: "Nowhere in the world have there been such firm consistent social changes as in Yugoslavia." And they justified modifying socialism to fit Yugoslavia's needs: "We study and take as an example the Soviet system, but we are developing socialism in our country in somewhat different forms. We do not do this in order to prove that our road is better than that taken by the Soviet Union . . . but because this is forced upon us by our daily life."

Impoverished Yugoslav children crouch on the floor of their dilapidated home while eating a meal of mush. After political pressure failed to topple Tito's regime, Stalin enacted a Cominform economic boycott in June 1948 that cut Yugoslavia off from its primary trading partners and exacerbated its already troubled economic situation.

The final break occurred when the Cominform, meeting on June 28 in Bucharest, Romania, voted to expel Yugoslavia from the communist movement and impose a complete economic blockade. Aside from armed intervention, economic pressure was the last weapon available to Stalin, but it was a strong one. Yugoslavia had depended on communist countries as the primary market for industrial exports and as an important source from which to import basic commodities like cotton and oil. Expulsion also meant the loss of mutual assistance treaties with Cominform nations.

Tito's reaction to the news was impulsive and somewhat bizarre: he grabbed his rifle from its rack, ran to his backyard pond, and shot all the frogs in it. But after regaining composure, he acted wisely and decisively, as he always had in times of crisis. First he assembled the central committee, which unanimously repudiated the Cominform resolution. Then, in a bold move, he published in the party newspaper, *Borba*, not only the Cominform resolution but most of the recent correspondence with the Soviet Union. Crowds jammed the news stands to read the remarkable documents. A tremendous rally of public support ensued, which carried over into the Fifth Congress of the YCP, held on July 21, 1948. There was some uncertainty before the meeting about how the rank and file of the party gathered there would react to Tito's defiance of a country they had long been taught was the repository of all true Marxist knowledge. But there was little question after Tito had delivered a tremendous eight-hour speech that encompassed the history of his devotion to the movement, nostalgic reminiscences of the wartime struggle, convincing rebuttals to Stalin's charges, and a comprehensive accounting of the party's achievements during Tito's 10-year period of leadership.

He sat down to thunderous applause and chants of "Tito, Tito." He had won a significant victory. He had rejected Moscow's claims to moral authority over the communist family of nations, asserted his nation's right to develop its own version of socialism, and resisted intense Soviet pressure to recant

> *I had to give Stalin time to behave in such a way that the people of Yugoslavia would say 'Down with Stalin' of their own accord without my having to suggest it to them.*
> —JOSIP BROZ TITO
> addressing the Fifth
> Congress of the YCP,
> July 1948

Tito (puffing on a cigarette held in a pipelike holder) poses with coal miners in 1949. His apparently carefree manner, coming in the midst of the threatening conflict with the Soviet Union, manifests the confidence with which Tito always acted. After the Fifth Congress of the YCP endorsed Tito's defiance of Stalin, the Yugoslav leader revived ties with the West to avoid political isolation and economic ruin.

However much each of us loves the Soviet Union, he can in no way love his own country less.

—motto of Tito's regime

his positions. Party representatives from throughout Yugoslavia had endorsed his actions. He had proven himself to be the true leader of his nation.

Slanders against Tito continued to appear in the Soviet press, but they only served to rally Yugoslavians behind their leader. By the end of 1948 it became obvious that Stalin's political pressure was not going to achieve its objective. But the Soviet leader had other tactics available. Over the next five years, several attempts on Tito's life would be made by Soviet agents. During this period Yugoslavian police arrested 12 Russians on charges of conspiring to murder Tito. The Yugoslavian leader was forced to live behind a massive security apparatus. Whenever he was scheduled to make a public appearance, secret police would scour the area, searching homes, setting up roadblocks. His aides went so far as to taste all of his food.

Yugoslavians also suffered terrible hardship as a result of the loss of commercial relations with Cominform countries — which had made up 55 percent of the country's trade. Rationing had to be introduced. Grain rotted in warehouses and produce withered on the trees for lack of foreign markets. Factories became inoperative for lack of foreign parts. In addition, the nation had to be constantly on the lookout for a Soviet invasion.

As he did so often in crises, Tito came up with an innovative and pragmatic solution. For his country to survive, he would have to put aside ideological considerations and revive relations with the West. As it happened, the West was equally willing to negotiate, believing that if Tito were overthrown, Soviet influence was bound to prevail in his country. Aiding Tito might also help loosen the Soviet hold over Eastern Europe by showing Cominform nations that there existed alternative sources of aid. Though the United States at first suspected that Yugoslavia's break with Moscow was a Yugoslav-Soviet plot to gain financial assistance for world revolution, eventually, on February 18, 1949, the U.S. National Security Council lifted a secret economic embargo, and a $20 million loan was authorized.

In spite of his country's dire need, Tito insisted that no political strings be attached to aid packages. He made it clear that he preferred not to be a stooge of either superpower. In the words of historian Phyllis Auty, "In order to emphasize that he was not a capitalist lackey, as Russian propaganda had often described him, he remained proud and distant and his officials were difficult to deal with." In the years between 1949 and 1959, Tito obtained $2.4 billion worth of Western aid—loans, surplus grain, medical supplies, military equipment, service aircraft, and credit for buying heavy machinery for industry. The United States was the largest contributor, even offering training for Yugoslav specialists.

Tito's next step was to reequip his army to make it secure against Soviet attack. The flow of funds from the West helped Tito keep his large standing army. An additional deterrent was provided when U.S. Secretary of State Dean Acheson warned Stalin that the United States would respond to any strike against Tito, and his warning was echoed by British Labor Minister Aneurin Bevan. In the end, Stalin preferred not to risk war by invading — a decision greatly influenced by the United States' status as the sole possessor of the atom bomb. Tito's independence was finally secure.

SOVFOTO

Joseph Stalin suffered a tremendous loss of prestige when Tito deserted the Moscow camp. The Soviet leader's unsuccessful campaign to remove Tito from power featured several assassination attempts and a propaganda war that called the Yugoslav, among other slanders, a "troubadour of Wall Street" and "an insolent dwarf."

10

Titoism

Yugoslavia's breach with Moscow would ultimately have a profound impact on international politics. It would completely transform American
perceptions of the communist world, undermining
the previous assumption that communism was a
monolithic structure, showing that not all communist countries took orders from the Soviet
Union. It would suggest to American leaders that
they could cope with communism's perceived threat
by encouraging — through programs of aid and
trade — other Iron Curtain nations to seek greater
independence from Moscow. At the same time, the
notion that innumerable roads to socialism were
conceivable would breathe new life into foundering
socialist movements in Western Europe and the
Americas. The breach would also inspire movements toward greater national autonomy in other
Eastern European countries, influencing unsuccessful rebellions in Hungary and Poland in 1956
and in Czechoslovakia in 1968.

Escaping the Soviet Union's dominance enabled
Yugoslavia to establish without interference its own
foreign-policy agenda, to institute new economic
programs, and to reevaluate political concepts. Tito's new contacts with the West led him to jettison
the Leninist idea that conflict was inevitable between capitalism and communism. World peace became the cornerstone of Tito's foreign policy.

> We say that socialism cannot
> be built with bayonets, cannot
> be built by administrative
> measures. It can be built
> only with the consciousness
> of the people.
> —JOSIP BROZ TITO

**Winning independence from Moscow enabled Tito to
modify socialism in accordance with Yugoslavia's own
needs and traditions. The result, a system called "Titoism," was characterized by reduced political repression
and a decentralized economy in which workers were
given an expanded role in management.**

Ultimately, the break with Moscow forced Yugoslavian leaders to reexamine the fundamental goals of their communist state, to look more closely at a system they had borrowed almost in its entirety from the Soviets. Did communism exist for the good of the people or to perpetuate its own existence? They chose the former, electing to get rid of many of the coercive aspects of the system and to strive toward the Marxist-Leninist ideal rather than the Stalinist one.

A gradual thaw, a relaxation of political repression, accompanied these ideological adjustments. After 1949, individual citizens experienced much less interference by the state in their lives. The secret police became much less aggressive. In the economy, elements of capitalism became prevalent. The government abandoned its enforced collectivization program for agriculture—which had brought about hardship and economic failure. By 1953, peasants privately owned 80 percent of Yugoslavia's farmland. To comply more closely with Marx's dictum that, in communism, the means of production should be owned by the proletariat, the central bureaucracy relinquished much of its control of industry. A law passed in 1950 established that each factory would have a workers' council with power to shape all decisions, including the division of profits. The institution of worker self-management became a cornerstone of the Titoist system and one of its primary contributions to the history of economic thought. To the extent that state planning remained, it was decentralized, with responsibility passing from the central authority in Belgrade to bureaus in the six federal republics.

These changes in part reflected Yugoslavia's new receptivity to the influence of Western ideas and its desire to mollify Western critics in the interest of keeping aid flowing. But in general the new system, which eventually became known as Titoism, reflected the Partisan tendency to be pragmatic, incorporating attractive aspects of East and West to suit the needs of Yugoslavian communism.

The trend toward democratization and liberalization continued with the Sixth Party Congress of the

YCP, held in Belgrade in November 1952. Resolutions passed at the meeting pronounced the YCP the only true exponent of Marxism-Leninism and called the Soviets the "worst kind of imperialists" and "state capitalists." Changing its name to the League of Communists, the YCP agreed to limit itself to an advisory and educational role — as opposed to an executive one. "From now on, the party line is that there is no party line," politburo member Milovan Djilas said.

These reforms were incorporated into a new constitution — passed in January 1953 — which also changed Tito's title from prime minister to president and transferred a great deal of authority to local governments, called communes, which would administer health care, education, arts programs, and other social services. As time went on, political strictures were further relaxed. Yugoslavians were given the right to criticize Tito's regime and were allowed complete freedom to travel abroad. "You have only to go into the countryside to hear people criticizing freely," Tito told foreign journalists in 1953. "We are not afraid of criticism, and we don't stifle it. We openly admit it when we have made a mistake." As the arbitrary powers of the police were reduced, a new penal code was instituted, and the legal system was revamped, allowing accused criminals to be considered innocent until proven guilty.

The differences between Yugoslavia's new system and the coercive, repressive Soviet form of communism were duly noted by Western observers. Western leaders expressed support for Tito's reforms and extended offers of further cooperation. In 1951 Tito concluded a military assistance pact with the United States. Relations even improved with the government of Greece, against whom Tito had funded a communist rebellion during the 1940s. In 1953 Tito signed a mutual-defense agreement with Greece and Turkey, both members of the North Atlantic Treaty Organization (NATO), a defensive alliance formed by many of the Western nations. Tito's rapprochement with the West reached its climax in March 1953 when he visited Great Britain. It was his first trip to a noncommunist country

> *Things have changed since the Bolshevik revolution. Nations of the West are moving leftward too. There is a possibility that instead of clashing they will one day come together in common agreement.*
> —MOŠA PIJADE
> member of the Yugoslav politburo, speaking to American journalist in 1950

Soviet tanks rumble through Budapest, Hungary, in autumn 1956. The Soviet Union sent 12 Red Army divisions into the Hungarian capital to remove from power a rebel government that had introduced liberalizing reforms similar to those instituted by Tito. Hungary was only one of many Soviet satellites whose leaders were inspired to seek greater independence from Moscow in the wake of Tito's successful defiance of Stalin.

since 1944. Tito was accompanied by his third wife, Jovanka Budisavljević, a tall, handsome Serbian woman 32 years his junior, whom he had married after divorcing his wartime companion, Herta Has. Jovanka had lost most of her family in World War II, in which she had fought as a Partisan. Tito's itinerary included dinner with British Prime Minister Winston Churchill and lunch with Queen Elizabeth II. "Imagine a communist who was once a peasant lad in the mountains fighting his brothers for enough bread to stay alive, breaking bread with the queen of England in Buckingham Palace," Tito later commented to an aide.

While Tito was en route to London he received the shocking news that his longtime adversary Joseph Stalin had died on March 5, 1953. Upon his return to Belgrade, Tito received several messages from the Soviet Union's new leaders, saying that they were hopeful of reestablishing relations with Yugoslavia. The Yugoslav leader who had fought so hard for his country's independence was understandably slow to respond. He was especially worried that reviving ties with the Soviet Union would jeopardize his valuable economic contacts with the West. After thinking the offer over, Tito agreed to once again exchange ambassadors and to resume trade on a limited basis — but that was as far as he would go. Nikita Khrushchev, who would eventually win the power struggle for Stalin's vacated position, reinforced the new Soviet line by enthusiastically welcoming the Yugoslav ambassador to Moscow and extending an invitation for "Comrade Tito" to visit the Soviet Union himself. Khrushchev considered it crucial to win Tito back into the fold in order to offset the challenge to Soviet authority then being made by another communist nation, the People's Republic of China.

Though Tito was not excited by the prospect of traveling to Moscow, he did invite Khrushchev to Belgrade in May 1955. Insisting that "everything is going to be all right," the first secretary of the Soviet Communist party stepped off his plane at the Belgrade airport, immediately grabbed a microphone, and issued profuse apologies for Stalin's campaign against the Yugoslavs. Khrushchev blamed the breach on "enemies of the people" who had since been eliminated from the Soviet Union; he concluded his speech by exclaiming, "Long live Tito, Long live Yugoslavia." An unsmiling Tito simply showed Khrushchev to the waiting limousine. For the next week the two leaders held a series of meetings in which discussions often became quite heated. When the dust cleared, Tito had won an enormous victory: the Soviets signed a joint communiqué in which they agreed that "questions of internal reorganization or differences of social system are solely the concern of the individual countries." At Tito's insistence, the agreement was signed not by Khrushchev, the party secretary, but by Nikolai Bulganin, the Soviet premier, symbolizing that it was a pact between independent states, not communist parties. After penitently coming to Yugoslavia to seek forgiveness, the Soviets had not only acknowledged Tito's right to political independence, but they had also seemed to abandon their previous claims to absolute authority over all communist nations.

Over the course of the next year, Tito used his new power with the Soviets to gain several additional concessions. Khrushchev acceded to Tito's demands that economic cooperation be restored between Yugoslavia and Soviet satellites, that the Cominform be disbanded, and that Yugoslav citizens imprisoned by Stalin be released. In early 1956 Khrushchev himself seemed to be moving toward Titoism, as he condemned Stalin's brutal rule in a

We really knew that we had come to a friendly and allied country. . . . We found a common language in all matters. We were treated as equals and not with the arrogance we saw in the East.
—JOSIP BROZ TITO
on his visit to
Great Britain in 1953

UPI/BETTMANN NEWSPHOTOS

Milovan Djilas, a Montenegrin lawyer who had joined Tito's politburo in 1940 and become its leading theorist, was relieved of all government posts in early 1954 after criticizing the party for corruption and enjoyment of special privileges. Imprisoned twice during the next two decades, Djilas became Tito's most relentless critic.

speech before the 20th Congress of the Soviet Communist party and initiated a gradual easing of political repression in his country known as the "Great Thaw." Tito's reconciliation with the Soviet Union culminated in his 1956 trip there. At every stop on his tour, Tito was greeted by huge crowds that turned out to cheer for his renewed friendship with the Kremlin and signal their approval of his heroic stand against Stalin.

Though Tito and Khrushchev spoke in Moscow of a "broad similarity of views" on several topics, the resumption of close relations by no means meant that Yugoslavia had rejoined the Soviet bloc. At the same time, Yugoslavia kept its distance from the capitalist West. On one occasion, Tito lashed out at NATO, saying that the military alliance had been rendered unnecessary by the replacement of Stalin with more reasonable leaders. Tito also criticized the United States for military maneuvers made in support of Chiang Kai-shek and his Taiwan-based Nationalist troops in their attempt to recapture the Chinese mainland from the People's Republic of China.

Tito realized that he could win valuable economic and military support from both major power blocs—and increase his own power—by playing each side in the Cold War against the other. He also recognized that many other young, developing nations, many of which had recently won independence from colonial powers, had similar desires to avoid being drawn into alliance with either the Soviet Union or the United States. Seeking to strengthen ties with some of these "nonaligned" nations, Tito visited India, Ethiopia, and Egypt in 1955. He hoped to organize these countries — "Yugoslavia's true allies and greatest friends"—into a Third World force, one that could preserve peace between the superpower blocs by remaining neutral. In 1956 Tito invited Egypt's President Gamal Abdel Nasser and India's Prime Minister Jawaharlal Nehru to visit him at his summer home on the island of Brioni. At this meeting, the three leaders founded a league for nonaligned nations. They pledged their commitment to peaceful coexistence between nations, disarmament, and an end to power blocs. After recruiting several other countries for the nonaligned movement, Tito hosted its first formal gathering. From September 1 to September 6, 1961, leaders from 25 states gathered in Belgrade for talks.

While in the area of international affairs Tito had succeeded during the 1950s in greatly enhancing his nation's prestige, domestically his regime had been rocked by intraparty conflict. As Tito encouraged Yugoslavians to evaluate his government honestly, Milovan Djilas warned that rather than fulfilling Marx's prediction of a classless society, Yugoslavia had in fact developed a new class — party functionaries. In 1953 Djilas began publishing a series of articles in *Borba* in which he criticized Yugoslavia's failure to transfer fully authority over economic enterprises to the workers. "If the revolution is to survive, it must transform itself into democracy and socialism," he wrote. Though the articles produced a storm of controversy, Tito encouraged Djilas to keep writing — that is, until Djilas published a stinging satire of party life in Yugoslavia. With this article Djilas had gone too far, and the central committee forced Tito to allow a trial of Djilas, which began on January 16, 1954. Djilas was stripped of all his government posts and retired to his home as a private citizen. He would later be jailed in 1956, after a further crisis broke out over an interview he gave to *The New York Times* and over his condemnation of Tito's noncommittal response to the Soviet Union's brutal repression of the 1956 rebellion in Hungary.

Perhaps as a consequence of the Djilas controversy, Tito in the early 1960s pressed for greater economic reform and political liberalization. In 1963 he released 2,500 political prisoners. Upon examining the progress of his economic revolution, he had discovered many bureaucratic errors and governmental injustices. To correct the errors, Tito continued in the direction that in the 1950s had produced a huge economic boom — decentralization. Further power was given to workers' councils to manage industry, and, to a much greater extent, market forces, rather than centralized planning,

May Day parade in Belgrade in 1964. A year earlier Tito had been elected president of Yugoslavia for life, and he remained president of the Communist party.

EASTFOTO

> *Communism really exists nowhere, least of all in the Soviet Union. Communism is an ideal that can be achieved only when people cease to be selfish and greedy and when everyone receives according to his needs from communal production. But that is a long way off.*
>
> —JOSIP BROZ TITO

were allowed to dictate the prices of goods. Apartment houses were given over to tenant councils; local governments were given far greater responsibility for taxing and planning.

In 1965 a depression made some party members doubt the worth of the new reform program of increased decentralization. By the second half of the year, forces within the party had effectively stalled Tito's program. They were led by Aleksander Ranković, head of the security apparatus and Tito's likely successor. When Tito learned that his own house had been bugged by Ranković's henchmen, he called a special meeting of the central committee. Not only had Ranković opposed Tito's economic plans, but he had also grown too powerful. In addition to having access to all classified secret police data, Ranković, as organizing secretary of the party, controlled all political appointments. In Tito's words, "He had the entire party in his hands." Though in view of his war record Ranković was not charged with any crimes against the state, he was removed from office and pensioned out of public life.

Relations with the Soviet Union continued to swing back and forth. The pattern had been established as far back as 1956 when, after Tito's visit to Moscow, the nations clashed over the harsh Soviet response to the uprising in Hungary and over Yugoslavia's support of the Polish leader Wladyslaw Gomulka, who had followed Tito's lead in telling the Soviets that "every country has a right to be independent." A reconciliation in 1957 had quickly been followed in 1958 by Khrushchev's pronouncement that Tito was a "Trojan Horse" and that the 1948 Cominform resolution to expel Yugoslavia had been "fundamentally correct." This seesaw pattern continued throughout the 1960s, a period during which Yugoslavia attempted to establish itself as a force for peace in Eastern Europe. In 1963 Yugoslavia and Romania signed a joint proclamation urging that the Balkans be transformed into an area free of nuclear weapons. In 1964, when the Soviet Union and Romania were on the verge of war, Tito helped defuse the crisis.

In June 1967 Tito appeared to move closer to the Soviets when he followed their lead in aligning with Egypt during the Arab-Israeli Six-Day War. But then, in August 1968, Soviet troops invaded Czechoslovakia in response to a local campaign of reform called by Czech leader Alexander Dubček, "communism with a human face." Worried that Yugoslavia might face similar treatment, Tito immediately condemned the occupation. Soviet leader Leonid Brezhnev warned that the Red Army would not hesitate to conduct similar interventions in other communist countries where it saw evidence of too much liberalization (a policy known as the "Brezhnev Doctrine" that would later come to bear in the Soviet invasion of Afghanistan in 1979). As an outgrowth of the Czechoslovakian crisis, Yugoslavia formed a territorial defense force, designed to carry on a guerrilla war should the Red Army overthrow Yugoslavia's central government and defeat its conventional forces. In addition, Yugoslavia and Romania pledged to work together to repel any future Soviet attack on either nation.

During the 1970s the most pressing problem confronting Tito was the reemergence of disputes between Yugoslavia's diverse ethnic groups. Decentralization had resulted in unequal distribution of economic advancement, reviving old hatreds and jealousies that many thought had been eliminated. On the one hand, the relatively less developed republics of Macedonia and Montenegro in the south resented the higher standard of living enjoyed by the northwestern republics of Slovenia and Croatia. On the other hand, northwesterners disliked having to subsidize growth in poorer regions. There were also political, linguistic, and economic conflicts between the largest and most powerful provinces, Croatia and Serbia.

Tito was especially disturbed by the rise of a strong separatist movement in his home province of Croatia. Over the course of a few months in 1971, membership in Matica Hrvatska, a Croatian social and political club, grew from 2,000 to 40,000. On November 22, 1971, students in Zagreb went on

An elderly Slav, dressed in traditional Serbian clothes and bedecked in medals from both world wars, salutes as he passes by Tito's coffin in Belgrade's parliament building. Tito died in Ljubljana on May 4, 1980, after a long illness. His funeral was attended by leaders from all over the world.

Jovanka Budisavljevic, a former Partisan fighter who became Tito's third wife in 1952 at the age of 28. Tito's marriage to a woman about 30 years his junior was thought by some to be an example of his belief in liberal social values.

strike for greater political and economic autonomy for Croatia. In response, Tito gathered together leaders of the Croatian Communist party apparatus and lambasted them for "rotten liberalism" in allowing such counterrevolutionary behavior. He then forced them to purge from their leadership key figures in the nationalist movement. To keep proper balance, Tito also conducted a purge of the Serbian party organization in 1972 and 1973: Thereafter, separatists turned to more extreme measures. Croatian terrorists blew up a Yugoslavian airliner in flight in 1972, hijacked an American commercial jet in 1976, and took over the West German consulate in Chicago in 1978.

Internal strife and a rise in domestic dissent forced Tito to wonder whether after his death the country would be wrenched apart by civil war. In 1974 he made arrangements for his succession. A new constitution passed that year named him as president for life and reinforced a 1971 law that had created a nine-member collective presidency to take over after his death. The collective body was made up of the president of the League of Communists and one representative from each of the six republics and from the two autonomous provinces. Members of the group were to rotate in Tito's position as head of state.

In May 1977 Tito turned 85. During the birthday celebrations his wife, Jovanka, attractive and elegantly dressed, was at his side. She seemed smilingly affectionate with the husband to whom she had been married for 25 years. But soon afterward it was noted that she no longer appeared at official functions. She did not accompany him when he traveled to Moscow and the Far East.

Tito and Jovanka had no children. But Tito was not without other family. He frequently saw both his sons and their wives and children. He spoke often of the joy his grandchildren gave him.

Tito and Jovanka had lived well, whether in one of the leader's many villas, on his private railroad train, or his own island. Even well into his eighties, Tito enjoyed speeding about in his convertible, dancing with beautiful women, and smoking expensive cigars.

As Jovanka faded away into the background, rumors surfaced that Tito was interested in another woman, sometimes said to be an opera singer, sometimes said to be a manicurist. There were other stories that Jovanka had plotted with Serbian generals to usurp her husband's office. Tito tried to squash the rumors, but as always he did not duck the question when he was asked directly. As one questioner persisted in trying to discover what had happened to Jovanka, Tito abruptly ended the discussion by snorting that Jovanka got on his nerves.

Age, however, was beginning to tell. Tito's health began to fail. He underwent several operations, even the amputation of a leg, as he battled cancer.

Then, one evening early in May 1980, Yugoslavians heard the announcement of Tito's death, just a few days before his 88th birthday. Citizens of the country he loved watched as his body was carried in his private railroad car to Belgrade. More than 120 heads of government attended his funeral. Tito's coffin was carried out of the parliament building, where it had lain in state, and placed on a gun carriage for the final trip to his villa. Leading the cortege were Partisan veterans wearing the blue and white ribbons of the medals they had won for gallantry in action. With them marched veterans of the Proletarian Brigades carrying the groups' original banners. Weeping thousands filed slowly through the streets of the capital.

Britain's Queen Elizabeth was just one of many world figures who sent tributes. Tito, she said, was "a great patriot and a man of outstanding courage and tenacity." Tito had left a legacy to his countrymen of independence. On a wider scale, he had shown other small nations that they too could walk freely among the great powers and perhaps keep them from starting a global conflict. These were no small accomplishments.

Tito salutes the armed forces during a 1975 parade marking the thirtieth anniversary of the country's liberation. Tito understood his unique place in Yugoslav history. Wanting to avoid a struggle for power after he passed from the scene, he left behind a collective presidency whose nine members now rotate Tito's former position.

Further Reading

Archer, Jules. *Red Rebel: Tito of Yugoslavia.* New York: Julian Messner, 1968.

Auty, Phyllis. *Tito: A Biography.* New York: McGraw-Hill Book Company, 1970.

Christman, Henry M., ed. *The Essential Tito.* New York: St. Martin's Press, 1970.

Dedijer, Vladimir. *Tito.* New York: Simon and Schuster, 1953.

Deutscher, Isaac. *Stalin: A Political Biography.* New York: Oxford University Press, 1967.

Djilis, Milovan. *The New Class: An Analysis of the Communist System.* New York: Praeger Publishers, 1957.

Djilas, Milovan. *Tito: The Story from Inside.* New York: Harcourt Brace Jovanovich, Inc., 1980.

Maclean, Fitzroy. *Josip Broz Tito: A Pictorial Biography.* New York: McGraw-Hill Book Company, 1980.

Singleton, Fred. *Twentieth-Century Yugoslavia.* New York: Columbia University Press, 1976.

Chronology

May 25, 1892   Born Josip Broz in Kumrovec, Croatia

1907–13   Travels around the Austro-Hungarian Empire, working odd jobs

June 28, 1914   Gavrilo Princip, a Serbian nationalist, assassinates Franz Ferdinand, heir to the Austro-Hungarian throne, sparking World War I

1915   While fighting for the Austro-Hungarian army, Broz is wounded and taken to Russia as a prisoner of war

Nov. 1917   The Bolshevik party, led by V.I. Lenin, seizes power in Russia; Broz is freed and fights in the Russian civil war

1920   Broz returns to Yugoslavia

1921   Joins the newly formed Yugoslav Communist party (YCP)

1927   Appointed YCP secretary to the Zagreb branch of the Metal-workers Union (his first full-time party post)

1928–34   Imprisoned for subversive activities

1935–37   As high official in the YCP, assigned to Moscow to work for the Balkan secretariat of the Communist International; begins to use the name Tito

1938   Made secretary general of the YCP during second trip to Moscow

April 6, 1941   The Nazis invade Yugoslavia

June 1941   Tito forms a guerrilla army to resist the Nazi occupation

Nov. 26, 1942   Founds the Anti-Fascist Council of Yugoslavia (AVNOJ)

Nov. 1943   Establishes a communist government, the National Liberation Committee, and is proclaimed marshal of Yugoslavia

Oct. 20, 1944   Partisan and Red Army troops liberate Belgrade

March 1945   Tito becomes prime minister in a provisional government combining communists and monarchists

May 1945   Attempts to annex the Italian port city of Trieste, precipitating an international crisis

Nov. 1945   Holds elections for the Constituent Assembly

Nov. 1946   Launches first Five-Year Plan

June 28, 1948   The Soviet Union and its Eastern European satellites expel Yugoslavia from the Cominform

July 21, 1948   The Fifth Congress of the YCP unanimously supports Tito in his defiance of the Soviet Union

1950   Tito establishes workers' councils, giving Yugoslav workers an expanded role in management

Jan. 1953   The reforms of Titoism are incorporated into a new constitution

Sept. 1961   Tito hosts in Belgrade the first formal gathering of nonaligned nations

1968   Condemns the Soviet invasion of Czechoslovakia

1972–73   Purges Serbian and Croatian branches of the party

May 4, 1980   Tito dies, aged 87, in Ljubljana

Index

Ruth Schiffman is a writer and editor who lives in New York. From 1973 to 1979, she taught mathematics in New York private high schools. She is also the author of *Turning the Corner*, a young adult novel published by the Dial Press.

Arthur M. Schlesinger, jr., taught history at Harvard for many years and is currently Albert Schweitzer Professor of the Humanities at City University of New York. He is the author of numerous highly praised works in American history and has twice been awarded the Pulitzer Prize. He served in the White House as special assistant to Presidents Kennedy and Johnson.